RELIGION

in

Relationships

PARENTING · MARRIAGE · FRIENDSHIP · ENEMIES
THE WORKPLACE · OTHER CHRISTIANS · THE WORLD

A COMPILATION

Pacific Press® Publishing Association
Nampa, Idaho
Oshawa, Ontario, Canada
www.pacificpress.com

Designed by Dennis Ferree
Cover illustration by Justinen Creative Group

Copyright © 2004 by
Pacific Press® Publishing Association
Printed in United States of America
All Rights Reserved

Additional copies of this book are available by calling toll free 1-800-765-6955 or visiting http://www.adventistbookcenter.com.

Library of Congress Cataloging-in-Publication Data

Religion in relationships : parenting, marriage, friendship, the workplace, enemies, other Christians, the world/[edited by Tim Lale].
p. cm.
Includes bibliographical references.
ISBN: 0-8163-2028-4
1. Interpersonal relations—Religious aspects—Christianity.
2. Interperesonal relations—Biblical teaching. I. Lale, Tim, 1964-

BV4597.52.R45 2004
248.4—dc22   2004044282

04 05 06 07 08 • 5 4 3 2 1

Contents

CHAPTER
1

People Who Need People

William McCall

Barbara Streisand recorded a song called "People" that became a hit in the sixties. The lyrics spoke of "people who need people." My brother-in-law hated that song. "What dumb lyrics," he said. "People who need people are not lucky. The lucky ones are the people who *don't* need other people." I understand where he was coming from. People can let you down. If you need other people, you leave yourself vulnerable to being hurt. But people who don't need people are soulless. If you armor yourself against hurt, you become unreachable by love. The danger of being vulnerable—of needing others—is great. So is the reward.

Consider the life of someone who tried to live without community. When I met him in Hawaii, Ron had lived for a decade without money, sleeping in abandoned cars or down at the beach. He had started his homeless journey living in Los Angeles, where he would sleep behind the dryers at all-night Laundromats. He had misinterpreted the Bible's statement about money and believed it to be the root of all evil, so he determined to live without it. One day someone gave him a plane ticket to Hawaii—just put it in his hand *gratis*. He got on a plane and flew there, resuming his homeless, scavenging lifestyle. He received no government assistance and didn't ask for charity. He lived from what he could glean off the land, including garbage cans. He could speak with enthusiasm about the great meals he could get simply by knowing where to look. He liked school dumpsters because the children would often throw away their lunches without even unwrapping them.

Ron may have been the most unusual homeless person I have ever met. He was not a drug abuser, and he would never touch alcohol. He was in the prime of life, with a healthy, well-muscled body. With clear eyes and a handsome face, he could carry on an intelligent conversation. He had formerly been a professional wrestler, and one might suspect he had a brain-bolt knocked loose in the ring. Nonetheless, he viewed his homelessness as a spiritual journey. Though he was a genial person, his life and spiritual journey was for the most part solitary.

Ron's pilgrimage is reminiscent of monks and other ascetics. While I was touring the Holy Land I was able to see a monastery from afar, carved out of the side of a cliff. There were half a dozen monks living there, but this was not solitary enough for one hermit. He had built a little shack on the sheer face of the cliff above the monastery. Our guide told us he never comes down for provisions, and he is totally dependent upon food and water being hoisted to him on a pulley from the monastery below. Without human contact, he spends his entire day (supposedly) in prayer and the reading of scriptures.

Such spirituality, though not without historical precedent in the Christian tradition, is foreign to the Bible. The gospel defines spirituality in terms of love and service, not in rituals and rites or even personal piety. Needless to say, a hermit's life misses completely the biblical concept of the community of faith.

The culture Jesus lived in was far more gregarious than ours today and involved far more social interaction. According to author Bruce Malina, being alone in the time of Jesus meant being in a group of intimate associates.[1] Being truly alone was totally abnormal. Notice the way the following texts use the word *alone*:

And when he was alone, those who were about him with the twelve asked him concerning the parables (Mark 4:10, RSV).

Now it happened that as he was praying alone the disciples were with him (Luke 9:18, RSV).

So you hate organized religion

Jesse Ventura, governor of Minnesota, caused a firestorm of protest by giving an honest interview. Forgetting all politesse and tact, he told *Playboy* magazine that religion is for "weak-minded people." (This from a former professional wrestler!) A fuller quote:

"Organized religion is a sham and a crutch for weak-minded people who need strength in numbers. It tells people to go out and stick their noses in other people's business."[2]

We could substitute the word *government* for the term *organized religion* in the above quote and make as much sense. Organization is always spoken of as a virtue until it is coupled with the word *religion*. If organization makes people less spiritual, we could all achieve saintliness by becoming disorganized!

People who say they dislike organized religion would find some sympathy from Jesus, because He too struggled with the sanctimoniousness of the established "church" of His day. Do you think religious people are hypocritical? Too critical? Tending to obsess on small matters? Too concerned with appearances? Jesus had those complaints over 2,000 years ago (see Matthew 23). In spite of this, by word and deed Christ showed He was building a new community—a community that would be based upon new priorities.

All the lonely people

All of us are lonely people at heart. All of us need love. Yet love seems to be the rarest of virtues. As the population of the world grows, we find ourselves struggling with the irony of proximity without community. Why is it that the fundamental human need for socialization—for community, for love—is so hard to attain? In our increasingly mobile societies, lifelong friendships are becoming scarcer. The perpetuity of a single marriage is something we can hardly take for granted anymore. And extended family? We can hardly hold together our nuclear families, let alone a community.

Could it be that our exaltation of the individual has been at the expense of community? Fritz Perls, the founder of the Gestalt school of psychotherapy, wrote a poem that expresses the hyper-individualism of Western society:

I do my thing, and you do your thing.
I am not in this world to live up to your expectations,
And you are not in this world to live up to mine.
You are you and I am I;
If by chance we find each other, it's beautiful.
If not, it can't be helped.[3]

God's plan for us is far more noble than "you do your thing, I'll do mine." Several times in the first few chapters of Genesis, the works of God's hands are called "good." The first thing that is called *not good* is loneliness: "It is not good for the man to be alone" (Genesis 2:18). As soon as Adam and Eve's connection with their Creator was severed, their relationship with each other was ruined. When questioned by God, Adam blamed his wife as well as God, initiating the first marital discord (see Genesis 3:12). In Genesis 4 we read of Cain killing his brother Abel. Separation from God and the striving for dominance led to murder. In Genesis 11, the tongues of mankind are confused, the communication breakdown is almost complete, and the human race scatters.

The Bible ascribes all human relationship problems to the result of our separation from God. Yet the very first act of the Holy Spirit is to stage an event exactly the opposite of the Tower of Babel. In Acts 2, people from various nations and tongues are brought together with a common understanding as a new community is born.

The concept of *sin* can be understood as *separation*. It is, first of all, a separation from God, but the separation does not end there. It brings about the end of true love and intimacy between people. It does not stop with individuals but proceeds to divide tribe against tribe, nation against nation, class against class. The irony of Jesus' statement that *any kingdom divided against itself will be ruined, and a house divided against itself will fall,* is that Satan's kingdom *is* divided.

The devil can only destroy, not truly create; sin only divides, never unites. Although evil agencies will form temporary alliances, these alliances never hold together for long. Only the Spirit of God can bring about unity. Only God can truly build the house that will not fall.

The religion of Christ did not envision people living in isolation from the group, but as a part of a new identity: the people of God. David Augsburger puts it so: "To speak of solitary Christians is biblical nonsense. The word 'saint' does not occur, but 'saints' is often used."[4] This spiritual communion, sometimes called the *Body of Christ*, was to be the fulfillment of gospel spirituality and the arena in which God's gifts were bestowed. M. Scott Peck sees the need for us to hear a different drum:

> *Trapped in our tradition of rugged individualism, we are extraordinarily lonely people. . . . We are desperately in need of a new ethic of "soft individualism," an understanding which teaches we cannot be truly ourselves until we are able to share freely the things we most have in common: our weaknesses, our incompleteness, our imperfection, our inadequacy, our sins, our lack of wholeness and self-sufficiency.[5]*

Only the Bible among all the holy books of the major world religions says, "God is love" and models that love with such down-to-earth, nitty-gritty reality as the life of Christ. New Testament religion is less concerned about ritual and more concerned with relationships than any other. Yet one of the great frustrations of the Christian life is that though we base our sense of values on love, a truly loving community can seem to be so elusive. Two thousand years after Jesus of Nazareth walked upon earth, the challenge remains for individual believers to see their relationship to the group and learn how to build loving communities.

The historical examples of the dreadful consequences of failing to nourish the interpersonal skills that build community are numerous. It seems easy for people to find reasons for hatred. Many people carefully nurse wounds and resentments against different ethnic groups. Often these date from grievances thousands of years old. Some years ago the world witnessed the terrible consequences of tribal warfare in Rwanda when simmering resentment broke out in ethnic slaughter. In 1994, Hutu troops, mobs, and militiamen began a genocidal slaughter of rival Tutsis that resulted in the deaths of almost a million people, including some moderate Hutus. The saddest part of this tragedy is that the perpetrators of these crimes were nominal Christians. They maintained a veneer of conversion without fully letting their new identity—an identity that would transcend earthly loyalties—mold their thoughts and behavior.

Unless we put an end to ethnic bitterness, we are all doomed. Unless we allow our spiritual identity to run deeper than our racial, tribal, or ethnic identity, we are not converted. Paul talked about a "ministry of reconciliation" in the fifth chapter of 2 Corinthians. This is to be the business of God's people, not only working to reconcile human beings to God, but reconciling people to people. We are to be the peacemakers that Christ said were so blessed (see Matthew 5:9).

> *Christ's love compels us, because we are convinced that one died for all, and therefore all died. . . . So from now on we regard no one from a worldly point of view. . . . If anyone is in Christ, he is a new creation; the old has gone, the new has come!* (2 Corinthians 5:14, 16, 17).

This "new creation" is the new people of God. It means an identity that transcends tribal and social barriers. There are no longer worldly distinctions such as Jew or Greek, rich or poor, Hutu or Tutsi, black or white. To hold on to such distinctions is to still cling to a "worldly point of view." All people are one in Christ Jesus (see Galatians 3:28).

This new perspective may be one of the most practical signs of conversion. If we have died to our old nature, why do ethnic loyalties hold us? Any loyalty above Christ is an idol. If we see anyone as other than children of Adam and Eve, we are unconverted.

What sort of community do you think Jesus wanted? We would be hard pressed to find a category of people Jesus didn't accept. He scandalized the religious community of His day by His acceptance of all kinds of outcasts. "This man receives sinners and eats with them," was a charge He did not deny, and, in fact, went out of His way to affirm (Luke 15:2, RSV). If "birds of a feather flock together," it would have been a source of frustration to anyone trying to understand who Jesus was by whom He associated with.

Was He a political revolutionary? One of Jesus' disciples was Simon the Zealot (see Acts 1:13). Zealots were political revolutionaries who advocated the violent overthrow of the Roman authorities. Revolutionaries hate collaborators. "Publicans" were tax collectors for the Romans. Most of them were corrupt, but they would have been hated for their cooperation with the Romans even if they were not corrupt. Matthew was a tax collector (see Matthew 10:3). How could Jesus keep peace with two disciples so opposite?

As if His acceptance of sinners was not radical enough, who could have foreseen His reinterpretation of the very nature of Israel? The mission of Christ was to "the lost sheep of the house of Israel," yet Jesus predicted the expansion of the mission to the Gentiles and by word and deed paved the way for the enlarging of Israel's tent. "Other sheep I have, which are not of this fold: them also I must bring" (John 10:16, KJV).

With our Western bias toward individualism, it is common for us to think of prayer as a form of meditation: a highly personal, individualistic thing. The New Testament, however, places the emphasis on prayer as an exercise in spiritual fellowship. For instance, the prayer Jesus taught the disciple begins "Our Father" (Matthew 6:9). Notice that all the personal pronouns in this prayer are in the plural—*our* Father, give *us*, forgive *us*, lead *us*, and deliver *us*. The prayer that Jesus taught us brings with it an awareness of community and our relationship to one another.

You cannot pray the Lord's Prayer and even once say "I."
You cannot pray the Lord's Prayer and even once say "My."
Nor can you pray the Lord's Prayer and not pray for one another.

And when you ask for daily bread, you must include your brother.
For others are included ... in each and every plea,
From beginning to the end of it, it does not once say "Me."[6]

Maybe it is because of Jesus' warnings about spiritual hypocrisy that we've developed a super-personal attitude regarding prayer. Jesus had warned about those who "love to pray ... to be seen by men." And then Jesus said that in order not to be like them, we should go into our room, close the door, and pray to our unseen Father alone (see Matthew 6:6). This passage was given simply to warn us about public displays of piety for the purpose of displaying our righteousness. Jesus prayed in the presence of His disciples. That is why we have those prayers recorded.

A little help from our friends

Communities are places where friendships are nourished. The word *community* is related to the verb *commune,* which means to share thoughts and feelings. In a real community, the identity of the individual is intertwined with the identity of the group, neither being lost in the other yet both related. Part of who I am becomes part of who we are together. The building of the community of Christ involves the exercise of all the graces of the Spirit. Christ's community was meant to be a school of love. We are to accept, encourage, and support one another in our spiritual journey.

Stephen Ambrose tells about the friendship between Lewis and Clark, the famous explorers who set across America to chart the western two-thirds of the North American continent and the vast extent of the tract of land known as the Louisiana Purchase. It is often called the Lewis and Clark expedition, but President Thomas Jefferson commissioned Captain Meriwether Lewis for the project. It was Lewis who insisted that his friend William Clark be recognized as co-commander of the operation. A divided command is "the bane of all military men," pointing only to chaos, but Lewis was determined to enter the expedition according to the rules of friendship. Though the co-equal authority was not officially recognized, it was practiced successfully by the two men.

The rugged and dangerous journey took more than two years, and the expedition suffered many hardships. Away from all the amenities of civilization, the group of thirty men had to care for each other. "Lewis pulled thorns from Clark's feet and bathed them." And when Lewis got shot in the rump because of a hunting accident and had to lie on his belly in a canoe for a month, "Clark washed the wound twice a day. . . and packed it with lint, to insure healing from the inside out."[7]

What Lewis and Clark had done, first of all, was to demonstrate that there is nothing that men cannot do if they get themselves together and act as a team. Here you had thirty-two men who had become so close, so bonded, that when they heard a cough in the night they knew instantly who had a cold. . . . .They had become a band of brothers, and together they were able to accomplish feats that we just stand astonished at today. It was the captains who welded the Corps of Discovery into a team—indeed, into a family. This was their greatest accomplishment.[8]

The last uncharted region of humanity is in the realm of human relationships. The world has seen kingdoms based upon possession and power. It has yet to behold a fellowship that transcends boundaries and is knit together in love. It was never the Great Commission simply to preach a message. Christ's orders were to "*make disciples* of all nations" (Matthew 28:19, emphasis supplied). This means the building of an international community in which borders and social status are irrelevant. The idea of the loving community is central to the gospel.

The final witness to the world is to be founded upon love revealed in community (see John 13:35). Never in its history has the church had the opportunity to do this on a fully global basis. God's end-time community will be a model of the Divine Ideal, representing every nation, kindred, tongue, and people, valuing all equally. Whereas the world is divided along cultural lines, the church will be an egalitarian society and as such, perfect for God's purposes. This is our challenge, our privilege, and our high calling.

In the final analysis, our loneliness can be regarded as a part of a spiritual calling, because the Bible implies that God is also lonely. He has created humanity for companionship. Have you thought of the implications of the fact that to love is a *command* of God? God has told us to do what all human beings deep in their hearts already long to do. He has made the principle of His character the goal of our existence. Let's look at what the Bible says about community building and see if we can find some helpful principles that will assist us in our quest for love. Not only will we see solutions for our own lonely hearts, but maybe we can find gateways to bring "all the lonely people" of the world into the loving community we have found.

Pastor William McCall shepherds the Canoga Park Community Seventh-day Adventist Church in Los Angeles, California.

---

[1] Bruce J. Malina, *Windows on the World of Jesus* (Philadelphia: Westminster Press, 1993).

[2] AP news story, *The Washington Post,* September 30, 1999.

[3] Quoted in *Homiletics* magazine, May 19, 1991.

[4] David Augsburger, *Communicating Good News* (Scottdale, Penn.: Herald Press, date unknown), 89.

[5] M. Scott Peck, *The Different Drum* (New York: Simon & Schuster, 1987), 58.

[6] A mailing from Omaha Home for Boys, quoted in *Homiletics,* vol. 6, no. 2, 29.

[7] Stephen E. Ambrose, *Comrades* (New York: Simon & Schuster, 1999), 103.

[8] Ibid., 105, 106.

CHAPTER
2

"Honor Your Father and Your Mother"

Wilma Kirk-Lee

We don't often associate the Ten Commandments with relationships. Some people see them as a list of "don'ts." Yet, if we look at the commandments through the eyes of a loving God, we see how we are to be in relationship to Him through the first four; the last six explain how we are to be in relationship with each other. God starts the first commandment of relationships with a promise—and that's exciting!

"Honor your father and your mother, so that you may live long in the land the Lord your God is giving you"(Exodus 20:12).

That sounds simple enough. Honor—just what does that mean? The Bible interprets itself and says, "prize highly" (Proverbs 4:8, RSV), revere (Leviticus 19:3, LB), and obey (Deuteronomy 21:18, LB). Today, we have no problem with defining the first two phrases; it is the last word, *obey,* that seems to give pause. Parents seem to hesitate when it comes to making their children obey. Modern thought says it is not good to make children obey; it might break their spirit. How does this line up with the fifth commandment? What do we do with the promise? Or is that promise valid today? Does the fifth commandment apply only in Old Testament times?

When we move to the New Testament, we find Jesus as our example. We find Him living in the home of Mary and Joseph, His earthly parents. What would His life tell us of honor for parents? There is very little said in Scripture about Jesus' early childhood. We do know that when He was twelve, His family went to Jerusalem to Passover as all good Jewish families would do. It would seem that the family of Jesus was normal. After the Passover, traveling home in a large family group, they had gone a day's journey before they realized that one of the children, Jesus, was not in the group. They retraced their steps and found their child, *teaching* in the synagogue among the elders. When they confronted Him with their worries, He countered with, " 'Why were you searching for me?' . . . 'Didn't you know I had to be in my Father's house?' " (Luke 2:49, NIV). Even though His mother did not understand what He meant, Jesus did not argue or talk back. He went obediently home. Verse 52 sums it up: "Jesus grew in wisdom and stature, and in favor with God and men." Here we see obedience to parents in the New Testament.

Honor is due our parents. After all, they did provide for us when we were helpless and could not do for ourselves. They put a roof over our heads and clothes on our backs and food on our plates. Parents are supposed to do that anyway, and they did. So, are *my* parents the only people who deserve honor? I don't have to honor any other older people? I don't have to listen to or respect or obey any older person because they are not my parents? The commandment seems to apply only to parents. We need to look closely at what God's Word says about honor to other people who are *not* our parents. Because honor is not just something for our own parents.

Since the Bible is a textbook on relationships, it is important to realize that the primary relationship is in the family. However, the relationship does not end there. We learn how to interact in our home, and then we carry those interactions wherever we go. Paul reminds young Timothy how he is to relate to his members who are older than he is. He encourages Timothy to honor older men as though they were his father, and older women as though they were his mother. When we learn how to honor our parents, we know how to honor those who are older.

Timothy was a young pastor, and he was hesitant to deal with all the members of his congregation. He needed the counsel and encouragement of Paul, his mentor, to know what he should do when situations came up in which he would have to deal with tough circumstances with members who were old enough to be his parents. Paul told him that he should be respectful, remembering that the member could be his mother or father, but that God had commissioned him to do His work. He must deliver the words of the Lord. "Don't be harsh or impatient with an older man. Talk to him as you would your own father" (1 Timothy 5:1, *The Message*).

Peter, in his counsel to the church (see 1 Peter 5:5), admonishes us to be good followers. Some of the translations speak to younger people. However, there are some translations that just speak to followers. Showing honor when *you* are not the person in power is sometimes a difficult role to fill. However, parents need to learn how to model giving respect. There comes a time in life when *"don't do as I as do, but do as I say"* is no longer effective.

Peter seems to be saying in this passage that it is important that you choose to be a servant. It is interesting that the word *submissive* is used here. Submission is something you choose. You choose what clothing you will wear, so you choose the clothing of submissiveness or humility. The consequences of not choosing to be humble seem quite daunting; God *opposes* the proud. The word picture here of God opposing or setting Himself against a proud person is powerful. Who would deliberately set out to have God as an opponent? Of course, no one thinks that they are proud, but if your behavior falls in the category of insolent, overbearing, disdainful, presumptuous, or boastful, then you have God as your opponent. Parents who allow any of these behaviors from their children are not teaching them to honor them as parents and deprive them of the privilege of receiving the promise of long living. They also teach children not to honor or respect any other adult or person in authority.

Sometimes it is easier to respect and honor other adults and people in authority than it is our own parents. Parents are not always the nurturing, caring, loving Christians they should be. They may not know the Lord for themselves. They may not have been shown the love and care that they needed when they were children, and so they do not know how to parent in a loving and caring way. They may not represent God's love that is full of grace and mercy. They may represent God as a father who throws lightning bolts and is ready to pounce on every mistake and never let any misstep be forgotten. How and why should I honor a parent like that?

This is where the grace of God shines through in our lives. When we experience God's love for ourselves, we realize that we don't deserve all the love and goodness He lavishes upon us. We realize that He sets us up on high places. He gives us a robe of righteousness, when all we bring to Him are rags of shame and guilt. He teaches us that we are children of the King. We grew up in an orphanage, and we have been taught that we have nothing and we deserve nothing. Yet, we are royalty. God's love makes us who we have become—people who are worthy of honor and respect.

The realization of our value to God makes us treat others with respect and value. We can honor our mother and father, although their treatment of us may not have been appropriate during our formative years. We now know that we have always had a heavenly Father who has always taken care of us and provided for all our needs. He has planted people along our paths just when we needed them, and all of our needs have been provided. We know that our parents need the same love and grace that we have found, and we may be the only ones from whom they will receive it.

The Christian path of honor and respect seems so easy. It is so simple to just read the words. This is what Christians do, and we all say we're Christians. But it isn't always easy. We honor our parents; we love them even if they were not kind to us when we were children—because we're Christians. But sometimes it takes more than determination and prayer. It takes a good Christian counselor because the pains and scars of abuse from childhood are so great that a person will need help to deal with all those issues. That's a part of watching and praying. It means that when you deal with the parent who may have hurt you, you can honestly say "*I forgive you.*" The consequences of their behavior may not allow the role of parent in your life, but it does not mean they cannot be honored. Honor can be given because they are older and deserve the respect that age gives a person in life.

Honor is often coupled with respect. As parents prepare children for independence, children learn to respect their parents. Parents earn this respect through their consistent living, their nurture, their willingness to apologize, and their sharing of their faith walk. It is amazing how parents often feel that providing a roof, clothing, and food entitles them to respect. However, the apostle Paul realized that parents must do more than just provide the basics: "Fathers, do not irritate and provoke your children to anger —do not exasperate them to resentment— but rear them [tenderly] in the training *and* discipline and the counsel *and* admonition of the Lord" (Ephesians 6:4, Amplified, emphasis supplied). God's way of dealing with His children is not one of discomfort, but tenderness. Respect grows over time as a child sees a parent living the Christian life before him. Respect is gained when the child realizes their parents are human, make mistakes, acknowledge their mistakes, both to God and to their child, and learn from the mistakes how to improve the relationship. When a child sees this in her home, she then knows how to interact with others and how to parent when the time comes for her to represent Christ in her own home.

The promise attached to the fifth commandment is not often thought about. Most people want long life—if it were as simple as honoring one's parents then everyone everywhere should be living a long time! However, that does not seem to be the case. Maybe honoring Mom and Dad isn't that easy.

How *long* do you have to honor Mother and Father anyway? When you're a child, it's understandable that you would honor parents, but when you're an adult, things change. I don't always want to do things the same way my parents did them. It doesn't mean that my way is wrong—just different. Does honor mean that I can have a difference of opinion, or do I always have to do what parents say? When God said leave and cleave, it meant a time of maturity and starting a new home. When two people create a new home, they blend the backgrounds of two people to make a new thing. It will not look like either home from which they have come. When parents come to visit, they will see things that may not feel comfortable because it's not like *their* home. Respect will allow the adult child to explain the difference and remind the parent that this is a new home, where different circumstances prevail. Honor means that when the adult returns to the parental home, the rules of that home are followed.

Honoring parents when the child becomes an adult sometimes means that the roles are reversed. As parents age, sometimes the child becomes the parent. In this sinful world, the process of aging robs parents of their dignity through illness. Parents are not always able to care for themselves because of physical or mental illnesses. Adult children who are committed Christians, will provide for their parents in a manner that allows for their parents to maintain their independence and dignity in the best way possible. This may mean managing financial affairs so that the parent can live in the home they are accustomed to for as long as possible; it may mean moving a parent into the adult's home, or it may mean providing assisted living for a parent who needs professional daily care. Honor and respect for parents extends long beyond childhood years. Parents are to be cherished and honored throughout their lifetime.

Adult children who have parents healthy and alive receive a rich blessing from the Lord. Their children reap a rich benefit in having a relationship with their grandparents and having the heritage passed directly to them from another generation. In earlier times and less industrialized countries, this transmission of family values and heritage was and is common. It is one of the things that become lost as families move and life becomes more hurried and less personalized. Today, grandparents are known by a lot of children through phone calls, emails, letters, and visits on vacations, if at all.

Christians know where the boundaries lie when there is a conflict between obedience to God and obedience to parents. We are called Christians because we belong to Christ. We honor our parents because we have learned about grace and mercy through the redemption of Christ for us. When we see Christ hanging on the cross for our sins, we realize that He loved us enough to die so we could live; then we know that we live and love for Him. We love and honor our parents because our priorities put Christ first. When parental requests conflict with the law of Christ, then "we must obey God rather than men!" (Acts 5:29). That does not mean we are rude or arrogant; it means that we humbly explain when we must follow Christ's bidding instead of our parents'. When our parents do not know Christ, our behavior may be the opportunity for change in their lives. No one is ever won to Christ through rudeness or a list of "don'ts." When Jesus walked the earth, He won people through His kindness and love. He touched people; He did not debate. Those are the methods we, as His followers, must use. Certainly, if we are honoring and respecting our parents, that is what we will do.

I have been blessed to have my own mother live past the Bible's promised seventy years. Recently, she moved to the city where I live. This is a new experience for both of us. I have not lived in the same city with my mother since I was married more than thirty five years ago. She chose to move to town because she felt the need to live near family. She is blessed with good health, and she lives in her own apartment, drives her own car, and can care for most of her own needs. We live in a large metropolitan area, and she does not drive on the freeways. So, there are some places she is unable to go. Her sense of direction is great, though; she can direct anyone where they need to go. It has required flexibility on both of our parts to adapt to this new situation. We have negotiated along the way when things have gotten awkward. I have adult children in the area who also have a relationship with their grandmother. My mother is the only parent my husband and I have between us, so the dynamics are quite interesting.

The interesting thing that has happened with my mother's arrival is the number of people who are a part of our "family" circle who have taken her as theirs. She is "Granmommy" to a lot of little children and young adults. I am touched by those who treat her with the honor and respect that is due a biological member of their own family. I watch them care for her as if she were their own. I realize that my mother will never be alone or uncared for within this community of faith. It makes my heart glad. I feel honored as a parent because others care for my mother.

God's plan for relationships is to be represented in families. He began with a family in Eden. Along with the Sabbath, family is one of the things we have today from Creation. We should cherish both of these precious gifts. Paul reminds us in Romans 12:10, "Love one another with brotherly affection [as members of one family], giving precedence *and* showing honor to one another" (Amplified, emphasis supplied).

The only way we can honor or give precedence to someone else is through the power of the Holy Spirit. It is not a human characteristic to put someone else first. The human tendency is to "look out for number one." Christians who have experienced the grace and mercy of God perceive how great the price Christ paid for their sins and know that they did not deserve so great a sacrifice. They look at their parents and remember the sacrifices their parents made for them, and find that honor and respect cannot begin to repay their parents for all their investment in who they have become.

This is the commandment to which God attaches a promise of long life—if you will just honor your mother and father. It sounds like a win-win situation. Of course, anyone who has walked with the Lord already knows that He always provides opportunities where you can't help but be a winner when you deal with Him.

In God's plan, children have a responsibility—honoring Father and Mother. Our society seems to think that the commandment is "honor your children." However, I don't see our society offering a promise of anything with "honor your children"! God says if you honor your father and your mother, you'll have a long life. When you read in His Word, you find the life He promises is life more abundantly. A life honoring children is one filled with grief, worry, and fear. A life nurturing children will produce children who will know how to honor parents. God created us with the ability to make choices. So, the choice is yours. Will you choose to honor your parents or your children?

Wilma Kirk-Lee is executive director of the Center for Family Wholeness in Houston, Texas. She and her husband have been married for thirty seven years and reared three children.

CHAPTER
3

Parenthood—Joys and Responsibilities

Wilma Kirk-Lee

I'm always amazed at God's generosity. He gives us children to train and nurture for Him, and He is not through with us yet! I don't know if I would trust anyone with such an awesome task if they weren't perfect themselves. Yet, God allows us to become parents while we are still becoming. How great is God's love for us. "Don't you see that children are God's best gift? the fruit of the womb his generous legacy?" (Psalm 127:3, *The Message*).

The anticipation of a baby brings such excitement. Everyone around the new parents gets involved. People want to know when the anticipated birth date is and what the gender of the baby is. There is lots of advice given and gifts begin to pour in and the new parents can't seem to pass a baby department without wandering in and picking up a little something. Everyone seems to vie to give a baby shower. There is a lot of joy to go around when the announcement goes out, "We're going to have a baby."

One would think that since there have been so many babies born, and it seems so easy—at least when you watch—that babies are the simplest thing to raise. Anyone can do it. Yet, if that is the case, why is the Bible replete with admonishment to train up children, to instruct children, to discipline children? There must be more to this child rearing thing than first appears. What is a parent going to do?

Where does a parent turn? Babies aren't born with an instruction manual.

Christian parents know that they have received a legacy, a precious gift. Any time that you receive something precious, you want to know how to care for it. A legacy implies that you must keep it and pass it along to another generation. How do you do that for a child? What is it that you must pass along? The Bible begins by telling parents they are to tell their children who God is. How do you tell a baby who God is? The first lesson a child learns about God is that He is trustworthy. She learns this because she learns that her parent care for her needs. When she cries, a parent responds. When she is hungry, she is fed. When she is wet, she is changed. When she needs the comfort of caring arms, the parent is there to comfort her. A parent can be trusted. So when Mommy or Daddy says that God is our Father, then I know I can trust God.

That is a powerful comparison to make. God is like my parent. However, the only parent that children know is the one that cares for them on a daily basis. If the parent is inconsistent, mean, or indifferent, then God must be like that too. Children don't think in the abstract; they are very concrete thinkers. So the responsibility to represent God falls on the parent. Who do your children think God is?

God asks parents to teach their children as they go out, as they come in, as they rise up, as they sit down, as they walk along the way. Some parents take that advice to mean they should always be quoting Scripture and listing all the things children should not do. I'm not so sure about that. I would like to think that our God is more practical. I think He meant, teach your children about Me by the way you live. Are you consistent in what you say and do? Is your life consistent with what you read and teach? Do you act one way at church and in public and another way at home? Do you go to church and praise the Lord, say "Happy Sabbath" to everyone, and come home and roast the pastor, deacon, elder, or Sabbath School teacher for dinner? Children see parents for who they are. They cut through the façade and reach the real person underneath. I remember teaching a Sabbath School class a long time ago, and one of the children told me, "My mommy said she doesn't have time to teach me the memory verse." I thought that was very interesting, since the parent was very busy with the youth of the church. This same parent was very active, trying to save all the youth of the church, but didn't have time to train her own child. The message she gave to her own child was that he was not as valuable as other people's children.

It is difficult in this day and age to be a parent. Sometimes parents are challenged by outside influences such as the media. Even if parents have chosen not to have a television in their homes, they cannot escape the influence on their children. Other children share their exposures with their peers. The computer is both a blessing and a curse. Children usually know more about operating the computer than their parents, and they go places in cyberspace that they should not go. How does a parent direct their steps? How does a parent lead them in the way that pleases the Lord? What happens in the home where there is only one parent? In some households, grandparents find themselves raising their grandchildren. Can you imagine the challenge they face, when the generations must learn to live in the same household daily?

One of the greatest challenges for the Christian parent is how to discipline. The question comes, What does the "rod" mean? Immediately the voices whisper, "That means spanking." Let's look at the "rod." The rod belongs to the shepherd. When you look at the shepherd of Bible days, he used the rod to control sheep. He could reach out and draw a straying sheep back to the herd. He could use the rod to reach a sheep that was in a difficult place. Sometimes he would use the rod to break the leg of a recalcitrant sheep, so that he could carry that sheep close to him until he learned to follow. The rod was used in a number of ways; the breaking was the last resort. The rod was definitely for discipline, but the root of the word *discipline* is *disciple*. *To disciple* means to "teach." Solomon tells parents they are to train, teach, discipline (*disciple*) their children. All of these require time, patience, and consistency. Parents have to be present and intentional to train and teach. By the way, discipline is definitely different from punishment. Punishment by parents is usually done when parents are tired, angry, or embarrassed, and it is not about helping children

25

learn. It's about parents and how they feel or how they perceive others think about them.

Discipline means that a parent knows a lot about the individual child. Since each child is different, the approach to discipline must fit the child and his or her temperament. There is no "one size fits all" for discipline. If you have more than one child, you can't think that what worked with one child will work with the next.

Parents also need to know something about themselves. Paul reminds parents that they are not supposed to exasperate their children (see Ephesians 6:4). When parents are not in control of their own emotions or have not examined their own agendas or are not consistent, then it is difficult for the child to understand discipline. Discipline is meant to teach a child to discern the difference between right and wrong. There will come a time when the parent will not be present, the child will have to make a decision for himself, and he will need to have an internal compass to make firm decisions. This is what discipline helps him to do.

Parents who know how to discipline also know about developmental stages. Children mature at different levels. Expectations for behavior have to be appropriate to the developmental stage of the child. It is unrealistic to expect a three-year-old to act like a five-year-old. However, we sometimes have those expectations. We expect that a three-year-old child will sit down, be quiet, and not fidget in church, just because we say, "Be quiet." That is an unrealistic expectation. Then when everyone turns and looks at our child being a child, we get embarrassed, snatch the child, and walk out. The child is bewildered because this is what she normally does, and she can't understand what is happening. Developmentally, this is what a three-year-old child should be doing. Parents need to be comfortable with the age and stage of the child, and they should not be intimidated by other people's lack of knowledge. They must advocate for our churches to become "safe" places for children to grow and develop in the Lord. It is not always about children's church—some of the adults need the discipline of growing in grace next to the children.

Since some parents don't have the privilege of living where there are multi-generational family systems, they don't have the benefit of knowledge that comes from time and experience. They may think that children are miniature adults and that they should behave just like adults. Some of today's parents are so young that they think babies are toys, so when the fun of dressing them and playing with them is over, they can't understand why they are still crying and won't just be quiet. This is the responsibility of parenting that no one really talks about. The other responsibility that no one talks about is the fact that parents are to work themselves out of a job as a parent.

Parents are to prepare their children to go out into the world as self-sufficient adults. This means that parents move from teaching that first lesson of trust in God to their children to having a complete faith in God for themselves. Just as parents have found it difficult to launch their children from their homes as financially and emotionally independent adults, they have failed to launch their children from their homes as spiritually independent adults. As children grow and mature, they should accomplish developmental tasks that prepare them for living independently. Healthy parents realize that children are a *legacy,* something that is handed on from those who have come before. Children are not possessions; at best they are lent to parents to train and nurture. That means God expects parents to prepare them to be sent into the world as representatives of His grace and mercy. True success comes when their children possess a steadfast faith in Christ and have a character and personality that makes them stand head and shoulders above others about them.

All along the stages of development it is important that parents lead their children to Christ. Parents often think that bringing their children to Christ is the work of someone else—the Sabbath School teacher, the pastor, or the church-school teacher. However, the Word of God gives clear instruction that the parent is the person instructed with this sacred responsibility. In Psalm 78:6, 7, God commands (not suggests) that parents teach their children so that "they would put their trust in God and would not forget his deeds." Parents have abdicated their responsibility to others and as a result, their children have not made the crucial decisions for Christ along the way that are important.

Part of helping children develop a personal faith comes from parents telling their own faith story. Parents sometimes feel that if they tell their own struggles, they will weaken their stature in their children's eyes. However, children will realize that it is all right to falter and that Christ honors sincere Christians in their walk with Him. They then know that He will help them when they fall and that He hears their cry when they call out for His welcoming arms. They know that the rod He carries will reach into those hard-to-find places and lift them up into His arms, close to His heart. Children need to hear the stories of their parents' growth in the Lord. This is a part of the legacy of faith. Telling the story of how the Lord brought them from where He found them and put their feet upon the rock where they now stand is exciting and makes the Bible real.

I remember hearing the lines from Edgar Guest's poem "Seeing a Sermon": "I'd rather see a sermon than hear one any day. I'd rather have one walk with me than merely tell the way." This is what children need. They need the model of the committed, intentional Christian life. Parents need to live before their children the life that they preach. Children need to know that the God they hear about is One who answers prayers when things are tough. He is One who receives praise when things are going well. He is also One who forgives when mistakes are made. The best way for children to learn these principles is through seeing parents living them. If they hear parents talking only about how they handle themselves when things get tough, why should the children turn to the Lord? When there are tight times and you choose not to return the tithe "just this once," what will the children do when they have to make the same decision? When you get a raise, will the Lord get the praise, or will it be just because you worked hard? When you make a mistake with your child, do you apologize?

What type of God is represented to your children when you say "our Father"? What decision for Christ do you encourage your child to make as she matures? How is your child's independent decision-making skill developing, or is your child still looking to you, the parent, for every decision? If you were not around, would you feel comfortable with the decisions your adolescent child would make? If you would feel uncomfortable, then you have not been parenting in the style that the Bible directs. You should be discipling your child in such a way that she will be able to hear the voice telling her, "This is the way, walk in it." She should not hear your voice, but the voice of the Lord, just as Samuel heard the voice of the Lord.

God entrusts us with children even though He is not through with us. I still stand in awe of His great trust in us. That is a great representation of grace and mercy. He doesn't wait until we have it all right. He doesn't say, "Well you blew it yesterday, so I need to see how long you can go without a mistake." He gives us children and says, "Train them up to live well and love Me." He *rewards* us with children. He allows us to make them a legacy. We can pass on to future generations the story of His love and protection for our family through our story of how God has led and brought us with our children. He doesn't ask anything complicated—just tell how He loves us! Just show our children His love by loving them.

Wilma Kirk-Lee is executive director of the Center for Family Wholeness in Houston, Texas. She and her husband have been married for thirty-seven years and reared three children.

CHAPTER
4

Marriage Is Not Out of Date

Mike Aufderhar

Marriage is *definitely* not out of date! Many visible indicators here in North America might lead you to believe otherwise, however. The divorce rate has climbed to over 60 percent. Prime-time television seems to portray and legitimize every kind of intimate relationship *besides* a committed marriage. Same-sex marriages are being fought for and legalized. The pornography industry, both legal and illegal, seems to be flourishing in spite of increasing efforts to contain and restrict it. "Political correctness" has verbally so sanitized sins against the institution of marriage that teenagers having sex before marriage are simply termed "sexually active." Even comic strips, cartoons, and jokes make fun of marriage as something out of date and impossible. The list of examples goes on and on. So how can we say that marriage is *not* out of date?

Even in a world where people thumb their noses at marriage in hundreds of ways, there are some people—even outside of conservative Christianity—who are recognizing that marriage really makes sense. Scientists of various disciplines from sociology to neurology are stumbling onto little clues in their studies that we were made for marriage. One scientist, digging into a relatively new study of one branch of the vagus nerve, was finding how closely connected this particular nerve is to known centers for relationship in the brain and body, and concluded simply that we are "hard-wired" for relationship. Other studies are showing that people who have committed themselves to the marriage vow are having longer life expectancies. In the political arena, judges, governors, and those managing the ever-more-challenging issues of social services, are promoting marriage-strengthening programs because they have found that better marriages ease their work load in the courts and welfare system. Diane Sollee has pulled together a "Coalition for Marriage" that has for the last eight years convened a "Smart Marriages" conference, gathering people from different disciplines, directions, and political and religious views who have one thing in common—they all believe that the institution of marriage must be strengthened and sustained in our society.

If thoughtful people of the "godless" society around us are convinced that marriage is not out of date, shouldn't we, who serve the unchanging Creator-God, be convinced that marriage is not out of date? Absolutely! God *made* marriage. He designed it, crafted it, planned for it, engineered it, and built it into our very bodies, psyches, and souls for the satisfaction, happiness, and health of humanity, as well as for the glory of God. There has been no "factory recall." The marriage institution did not have an expiration date on it. There are no "new and improved" editions making the original one obsolete. God made it perfect at the beginning, and under His blessing and guidance it can be a perfect blessing to humanity still. Oh yes, it is true that sometimes marriage seems to be anything *but* a blessing to humanity, but this is not because marriage has gone out of date. It is because human beings have gotten out of sync with God's original design.

Marriage in paradise

If we could have been present when "he spoke, and it came to be; he commanded, and it stood firm" (Psalm 33:9), our mouths would have been hanging open in wonder and amazement. We would have been shocked by the light, astounded at the separation of the waters and the appearance of the dry land, overwhelmed by the sun, moon, and millions of stars, stunned by the sudden appearance of fascinating sea creatures and beautiful birds, and dumbfounded by the vast array of animals large and small—all created to reproduce themselves in the most fascinating ways. I have no doubt that witnessing the God of the universe stooping to the dirt and getting His hands muddy as He formed the first human being in history would have left us speechless at the very moment He breathed the breath of life into the father of the human race. Certainly, watching the first surgery—a bloodless one at that—and the creation of an even more beautiful being would have left us unable to be any more incredulous.

But I wonder. I wonder if we would have had any ability left to even begin to comprehend the inconceivable ingenuity God poured into his next two creations. Sometimes we forget that Eve was not the last work of the Master Craftsman that glorious week. He went on to create two intangible works of brilliance that we sometimes miss in our recounting of the wonders of that week. He created the fascinating, intricate, most intimate, interconnecting relationship that can exist between human beings. He created marriage. And once the marriage was sealed and blessed, He introduced His second gift for relationships—the Sabbath.

Twin institutions for the glory of God

These two institutions transcend the wonders of atoms, electrons, molecules, cells, tissues, organs, seeds, brains, and brightly burning stars. Marriage and the Sabbath are not about a physical, touchable artifact of the Creator. They are about the invisible spiritual and social interconnection between beings. Their lack of physical substance, however, does not in any way diminish the magnificence created into them. These two creations of the sixth day (remember, the Sabbath began on the evening of the *sixth* day), when blessed by the Creator, can be a substantial benefit to humanity and bring great glory to God.

When Creator Jesus walked this planet several thousand years after Creation and He was asked questions about divorce, "Jesus pointed His hearers back to the marriage institution as ordained at creation. 'Because of the hardness of your hearts,' He said, Moses 'suffered you to put away your wives: but from the beginning it was not so.' He referred them to the blessed days of Eden, when God pronounced all things 'very good.' Then marriage and the Sabbath had their origin, *twin institutions for the glory of God in the benefit of humanity"* (Ellen G. White, *Thoughts From the Mount of Blessing,* 63, emphasis supplied).

As Seventh-day Adventist Christians, we have focused much of our attention on one of these "twin institutions for the glory of God." We have studied, explained, honored, and proclaimed the Sabbath. This has glorified God. And the Sabbath has been a tremendous benefit to humanity as well, to the extent that we have been able to experience the Sabbath not as a legal requirement for true saints, but as a time of rest and relationship between the Creator and the created.

But what about the Sabbath's "twin"? Have we maximized the "glory of God" and the "benefit of humanity" that the Creator intended for Sabbath's twin—marriage? I don't think so. Do we really grasp what God wants marriage to be for the blessing and uplifting of humanity? The untapped potential here is vast.

First of all, we have the current situation in which marriage has been degraded to an experience that often results in pain, abuse, and violence rather than benefit. This gives us the opportunity to apply God's grace to heal people from the misery of marriage gone awry. Even in Ellen White's day marriage was, in most cases, she said, "a most galling yoke." She went on to say that "the books of heaven are burdened with the woes, the wickedness, and the abuse that lie hidden under the marriage mantle. This is why I would warn the young who are of a marriageable age to make haste slowly in the choice of a companion" (*The Adventist Home,* 44). With this much woe "burdening" the books of heaven, we need to apply our best study skills to the institution of marriage and learn how to train, coach, and mentor people in finding God's healing—both for individuals and for their marriages. Just seeing the misery in so many marriages should pull at the hearts of those who follow the One who came to "bind up the brokenhearted" (Isaiah 61:1), and it should propel us into action for Him.

Second, even as we strive to rescue dying marriages and the people dying in them, we have the opportunity to repaint the positive picture of what God originally intended. We can cast a vision much higher than merely surviving marriage. We can go beyond just having a stable, lasting marriage. We can invite people to set their sights on *thriving* marriages—marriages that begin to experience the incredible blessings that God meant for husband and wife to know after becoming "one flesh." This is what will begin to bring glory to God around this creative work of art called marriage.

Thriving marriages

What does a "thriving marriage" look like? How does a marriage bring glory to the God who created marriage?

Sometimes when my wife and I talk to people about having thriving marriages, I like to ask the audience how many of them would be excited if I told them that one of our door prizes was going to be a Mercedes Benz automobile. There is usually quite an enthusiastic response. Sure, who wouldn't like to have a bright shiny new Mercedes Benz to drive around in? Who wouldn't enjoy that fresh new-car smell and the feel of soft luxurious leather upholstery? Who wouldn't appreciate the sound of a finely tuned engine purring quietly under the hood, but ready for powerful action as soon as you press on the accelerator? Of course, some visualize a large, roomy luxury model, while others picture the sporty convertible, but in either case it isn't hard to adjust to the idea of having such a wonderful automobile.

Then, once their imaginations have taken them to the height of anticipation, I ask them how they feel about my offer when I show them the most beaten up, broken down, rusted out, falling apart, smashed in, burned out, smelly, smoking 1966 Mercedes they've ever seen, and I tell them that *this* is the car to be given away? Obviously, the enthusiasm suffers an instant death.

Then we consider one more question, "If you were the designer, creator, and maker of the Mercedes Benz automobiles, how would you feel about having the second car in the illustration represent your creative work?" Naturally, no one would be pleased to have his or her expertise and workmanship represented by such a poor specimen of what the vehicle was originally created to be.

God is the maker of marriage. It should be obvious that broken-down, failing marriages do not bring honor to Him as the One who came up with the idea of marriage in the first place. Even one that is still "making it down the road" with fits and starts, jolts and squeaks, and occasional bangs does not necessarily honor Him. So what does the thriving, or "new-car," marriage look like? What does that marriage have to be like to show off God's workmanship?

One of the characteristics of such a marriage is seen right in the Creation story itself. It's a marriage in which the unique differences of man and woman are so nicely blended in their unity and oneness that it provides the best human picture available of what God is really like. In Genesis 1:27 we're told that "God created man in his own image, in the image of God he created him, male and female he created them." Man by himself does not reveal the full image of God because to get that full picture of what God is like, you have to have both male and female. Why? Because that's the way God chose to make it! The Bible doesn't tell us why He made it that way. It just says that He did.

Then He created marriage to be that institution in which the beauty of the harmonious blend of male and female can really be seen. So for starters, a thriving marriage will be one that portrays something of the image of God in the way that the male and female exhibit His characteristics in their connections with each other.

We could go down a list of the characteristics of God and ask how each would best be demonstrated in a marriage. Take grace, forgiveness, patience, mercy, faithfulness, or any number of other attributes of God. How does each of these look when displayed in the marriage relationship? When one messes up and does something hurtful to his partner, and his partner doesn't react in a mean and hurtful way but offers grace and forgiveness instead, God is glorified.

Does this sound like a tall order? It definitely is. Thankfully the God who created it like that in the very beginning says that even now "all things are possible" through Him. He doesn't expect us to achieve this overnight. He offers us the only thing that can really make it happen—grace. "The grace of Christ, and this alone, can make this institution [marriage] what God designed it should be—an agent for the blessing and uplifting of humanity.

"And thus the families of earth, in their unity and peace and love, may represent the family of heaven" (*Thoughts From the Mount of Blessing*, 65).

Since thriving marriages bring glory to God, they will be important not only to those who are married, or even those who are contemplating marriage, but also to all of us as Christians. Thriving marriages benefit all of humanity. God may want to bless you through growth in your own marriage, and if you're not married, He may want to bless you through someone else's marriage. As a single person, you may find appropriate connection and nurture in a family headed by a couple enjoying a thriving marriage. God may be calling you, whether married or not, to pray for and support others' marriages. As children of God who want to bring glory to Him, we will want to do everything we can as individuals and together as congregations to help marriages thrive in our churches and communities.

Marriage—till death do us part

Besides the grace of Christ, the ingredient most lacking in marriages today is commitment. Many, fearful of the pain of divorce, simply choose not to marry and yet want all the privileges of marriage. Others who do actually marry have watered down their vows to each other to try to leave themselves loopholes to get out should the going get tough. If you listen to the vows used at some weddings today you'll hear little more than "I do until … I don't anymore." "Till death do us part" seems a missing phrase in the vows of today.

A commitment like "till death do us part" is what creates the safety for the growth of a thriving marriage. Thornton Wilder, in *The Skin of Our Teeth,* expresses the value of the commitment promise this way:

> I didn't marry you because you were perfect. I didn't even marry you because I loved you. I married you because you gave me a promise. That promise made up for your faults. And the promise I gave you made up for mine. Two imper-

fect people got married and it was the promise that made the marriage. And when our children were growing up, it wasn't a house that protected them; and it wasn't our love that protected them—it was that promise.

God wants this kind of committed promise between husband and wife. The Bible says a man shall "leave his father and his mother, and shall *cleave* unto his wife: and they shall be one flesh" (Genesis 2:24, KJV, emphasis supplied). I believe the word *cleave* encompasses this kind of binding promise.

Sometimes we forget that "till death do us part" signifies an ongoing commitment. Real marriage commitment not only begins a marriage, but it also must stay current and will need to be expressed in different ways over the life of the marriage. There is a reason why vows have contained phrases like "for better or for worse" and "in sickness or in health." Real commitment may have to be restated and reinforced when the going gets tough. When one partner becomes disabled, the kind of commitment required may shift. When there is a loss of job, a loss of a child, or some other major life change, husband and wife may need to find ways to refresh their commitments to each other to strengthen their bond and remind each other that they are still committed "till death do us part."

Our great Creator made marriage to be an agent for the blessing and uplifting of humanity, and when we take it seriously and set our sights on having *thriving* marriages, we can bring glory to Him and truly "represent the family of heaven" to others. May God continue to grant the grace to move us ever closer to this goal in our homes.

Mike Aufderhar and his wife, Brenda, direct the family ministries department of the Kentucky-Tennessee Conference of Seventh-day Adventists, and he pastors the Middletown Seventh-day Adventist Church in Louisville, Kentucky.

CHAPTER
5

Friendship

Tamyra Horst

Every day we come in contact with people. Coworkers. Sales clerks. Drivers who cut us off. Doctors and others with whom we have appointments. Our boss. Clients. Acquaintances. Mentors. Church members. Buddies. Good friends. Best friends. Family. Our lives are full of people. But it's the time we spend with family and friends that we enjoy the most, laughing and talking with people who know us well. They love our little idiosyncrasies, our humor, and our history.

Many of the people we encounter each day are in our lives by chance or because of our jobs or needs in our lives. And we're born into our families.

But friends are different. Friends are in our lives because we've chosen to include them. They make our days richer and add an element of fun. They're there to offer support, encouragement, and a listening ear. They're the people we call to share our heartaches and our joys. We *want* to spend time with them.

Jonathan and David knew about friendships. They were an unlikely duo. David was a shepherd boy, Jonathan, a prince. Normally their paths would never have crossed, but God intervened. He brought David to the palace to work for Jonathan's father, Saul. David's music brought Saul solace when his heart was troubled. David's personality drew Jonathan to him. "Now when he [David] had finished speaking to Saul, the soul of Jonathan was knit to the soul of David, and Jonathan loved him as his own soul" (1 Samuel 18:1, NKJ). Jonathan loved David.

Friends love each other.

Not just when everything is good and life is happy. "A friend loves at all times" (Proverbs 17:17). Friends are there when life is great, when the sun is shining, the bills being paid, everyone healthy and happy. But friends are also there when life seems to be falling apart. When the pile of bills is higher than the checking account. When the doctor shares a devastating diagnosis. When we just feel blue and aren't sure why. Even when we need more than we can give.

David was in just such a place. He had come to the palace to play music for Saul, but now Saul was out to kill him. David was running and hiding for his life. And Jonathan was there. He helped hide David. He went to his father and defended David, risking his father's anger and ducking a spear thrown from his own father's hand (see 1 Samuel 20:33). Saying goodbye to his much loved friend was hard and full of tears (see verse 41), but Jonathan knew he had to do whatever was best for David. He helped David escape.

How could he be so committed to his friendship with David?

God was the bond between them. "God will be the bond between me and you" (1 Samuel 20:40, *The Message*). Jonathan and David's friendship was based not just on human love, but on God's love and their personal relationships with Him. When God is in our lives, He should naturally be in our friendships. When He is in our friendships, they will be stronger and cause us to grow stronger personally and enable us to remain committed to each other—and not just here on earth. With God in our friendships, they will last for eternity.

How does God make a difference in our friendships?

First, God makes a difference in us. As we come to know Him personally and intimately, He changes us. He strips away our selfishness and teaches us how to be more "other-centered" than "me-centered." He shows us how to care about others, really care about them. By getting to know God, we become more like Him. We'll become like Jesus, who showed us how to truly be a friend. Jesus showed us how to care about others through the example of His own life.

As He creates this transformation in us, we no longer look at people to see what they can give us. We don't base our friendships on what they can do for us. We build relationships with people and *want* to give them support, encouragement, caring, a listening ear, a shoulder to cry on. We find ourselves wanting to help others. We begin to understand what it means to really love our neighbor.

This heart change also takes away our need to compete with others. We don't have to compare ourselves to our friends. We realize that God loves us and created us to be who we are. As we rest in this belief, we can encourage the dreams of our friends—even if those dreams are similar to ours.

Jonathan and David could have been competitors. But while Jonathan's father seethed with jealousy over David, Jonathan didn't. He recognized that God had appointed David to be the next king, even though Jonathan was next in line for the throne. He graciously shared God's dream for David. In 1 Samuel 18:4 we find Jonathan giving David his robe "with his armor, even his sword, and his bow and his belt." In giving David these items, Jonathan was symbolically giving to David everything that the items represented. He was willing to give his place, his princely robes and the authority that they carried with them, to David. He knew God had a plan for David. He trusted God to have a plan for him as well. He encouraged David and supported him in every way he could. He was committed to David no matter what. He didn't have to compete with or compare himself to David. He could surrender the throne to David graciously and willingly because He trusted God to take care of him.

Jonathan gave David another incredible gift that could only come because of his own relationship with God. "Then Jonathan, Saul's son, arose and went to David in the woods and *strengthened his hand in God*" (1 Samuel 23:16, NKJV, emphasis supplied). Jonathan encouraged David's grip on God. David was hiding out in the wilderness, with Saul seeking him every day (see verse 14). And David knew it. He was hiding for his life. Jonathan went to David in the wilderness to encourage him, to remind him that God would deliver him. He reminded David that God's dream for him would come true—he would be king over Israel. "Do not fear, for the hand of Saul my father shall not find you. You shall be king over Israel, and I will be next to you" (verse 17).

With God in our lives, our friendships become more than just a listening ear or a fun time. Our relationships strengthen our grip on God. They cause us to grow—as individuals and in Christ. Proverbs says, "As iron sharpens iron, so one man [woman] sharpens another" (27:17). Our friendships are deepened, and we are challenged.

How do we "sharpen" our friends?

First by praying with them and for them. Prayer is such an amazing thing! It is one of the most important things we can do for others—especially our friends. Because we talk and share with one another from our lives, we know what to pray about. We know what's happening, what others are struggling with, what things are most important to them. We know the desires of our friends' hearts. We can lift these things up to God each day.

Just knowing that someone else is praying for you and the things that matter most to you can bring peace, confidence, and strength— a sense that everything is going to be all right. But then when friends pray together for one another, that makes it even better! To hear someone pray with love and kindness for you and your needs can not only encourage you but give you added strength to face your trials.

Unfortunately, we don't pray with our friends often. We feel awkward or uncomfortable suggesting it. We find it so much easier to say, "I'll be praying for you" or "I'll pray about that for you." It takes a little practice to say instead, "I'm going to be praying for you about this, but let's pray about it together right now." Stepping out of our comfort zone and praying together will not only deepen our friendships, but will strengthen us in our struggles as well. Whether we're in person, on the phone, or "chatting" through email, praying with one another can cause us to sharpen one another and add a sense of joy and strength to all that we do.

Because of God's working in our own lives, we can also offer each other unconditional love. Knowing that friends will not judge us or be critical of us, but will love us unconditionally, enables us to really share ourselves. We can be transparent with one another. It gives us a place to be able to confess our sins and struggles and ask for prayers for victory. It allows us to be ourselves and not worry what other people will think or what we need to do to please them. We know that they'll love us just the way we are, no matter what. These types of friendships are comfortable. We can relax and not "try." We can rest, knowing that no matter what we look like, what we say, or what we've done, we're accepted and loved.

We can also sharpen one another by holding each other accountable. While God doesn't use the word *accountable* in the Bible, He commands us to go to a brother whom we see in sin and talk to him about it. God tells us to confess our sins to one another, to encourage one another and build each other up. This is all a part of accountability—asking the tough questions. We can challenge our friends to make their decisions in God's will, not their own. We can help each other to live the life that God has called us to. It's not always easy, and it may take some effort, but we need to be held accountable in order to grow and change.

What about friendships in which God is not the bond? Should we have friendships with nonbelievers? If our friendships with others who love God deeply cause us to grow and sharpen our lives, do our friendships with people who don't love God adversely affect us?

The people we hang out with do affect us. Often we don't even realize how much. We begin picking up words they use, expressions that are theirs, and even habits. When my husband, Tim, began working with Ron, I could "hear" Ron in Tim's conversations—words he used, phrases he began saying. I have found myself picking up mannerisms of friends and talking like them.

That's why God cautioned us about choosing our relationships carefully. Second Corinthians 6:14 says, "Do not be unequally yoked together with unbelievers." The Corinthians reading Paul's letter had an instant visual picture of what this verse meant. Oxen would be yoked together for work. If one ox were stronger than the other, they would pull the plow at an angle, making all the rows uneven. If one ox were bigger than the other, the yoke wouldn't fit well and could rub sore spots on them and make it uncomfortable for the smaller ox to walk. The oxen needed to be about the same size, weight, and strength so that they would pull together evenly.

While this verse is often quoted in regard to choosing our marriage partner, it applies to all our close relationships. God wants us to choose our deepest, closest friendships in this way. He desires that our closest relationships be with those who will sharpen us, draw us closer to Him, and help us to grow into the people He created us to be. He would have us choose friends who share our love for Him and our values, concerns, and beliefs.

Does this mean that we can't have friendships with nonbelievers?

Absolutely not. God also commanded us to be a light for Him to others. We can't be a light if we're not willing to be a friend. While we can choose godly friends for our closest relationships, God also desires for us to befriend our neighbors, co-workers, and others whom He brings into our lives. It's through friendships that the Holy Spirit will be able to effectively reveal God and the gospel to others.

We do need to be careful and watch how our relationships are affecting our walk with God. If a friendship in any way detracts from a growing relationship with Christ, then we need to prayerfully consider what to do. We may need to end the friendship or cut down on the time we spend with that particular friend.

But God desires us to be friends with those who don't know Him. Friendships are one of the most effective means of evangelism. Jesus knew this. His life is an example to us today.

Look at the people Jesus associated with:

- Tax collectors—One of the most despised occupations of the day, tax collectors were well known for cheating and stealing. The Jewish people felt that Jewish tax collectors had "sold out," betraying their own people to the Roman rulers. They charged more than just the tax levied by the Roman rulers and lined their own purses with the extra money.

- Fishermen—Not high on the social ladder either, fishermen were often thought of as rough and uneducated.
- Prostitutes and sinners—Jesus was often accused of eating with those to whom "good" people wouldn't even talk. Eating a meal with someone showed that you accepted them. The church leaders couldn't believe that Jesus would eat with such people! They certainly wouldn't eat with them or talk to them, look at them or having anything to do with them. (They weren't revealing a loving God to their communities!)
- A Samaritan woman—This woman had three marks against her. First, she was a woman. Women were often treated more like property than people. Men didn't typically talk to women in public. But this woman was also a Samaritan. Jewish people avoided Samaritans. They believed that just to walk through the land of Samaria made them unclean, and they would walk two or three days out of their way in order to avoid going through Samaria. Not only was she a Samaritan woman, but she had been married five times and was now living with a man who was not her husband. Yet there was Jesus, sitting by a well in Samaria, talking to a Samaritan woman.

Jesus desired for people to know God. It was one of the driving forces of His life—to reveal God in a true way, helping people to really know God, and not just about Him, not just the rules that were sapping the joy out of people, but to know God—His salvation, His grace, His love. He lived His life in such a way as to reveal what God is really like. Through His relationships with others, He sought to help them grasp God's love for them. He desires us to do the same.

Jesus' example of friendship teaches us how to be friends with others as well. First, He met their needs. He knew that to just share the gospel with them wouldn't work. He had to care about them, eat with them, talk to them, listen to them, and heal them. If he provided for their needs, then they would be ready to hear about God.

It's an example we can follow. We can invite people into our houses for meals and fellowship. We can provide for needs that we're aware of. We can just listen. People are lonely for someone to care about them. In our busy world, our relationships have suffered. People have become too busy for others—even the important people in their lives. Barna Research found that the generation known as Baby Busters wants relationships: "Busters are more interested in being personally known and connected." People are hungry for meaningful relationships in their lives. We can meet that need, and by doing so, will have opportunities to introduce them to a God who can meet their needs in ways we can't.

That's what Christ did. His goal in befriending people was to reveal God's love and care through His own love and care. As a result, fishermen became pillars in the early church; a prostitute's act of worship became an example of worship down through the centuries; one tax collector not only repented, but paid back four times what he had falsely taken; and a Samaritan village came to know Christ as Messiah, not through His disciples as they walked through the market and bought things to eat, but by the words of a woman with a bad reputation.

Christ not only gave us an example of how to befriend others for God, but He calls us *His* friends (see John 15:15). He didn't call us servants, though that's often what we try to be—putting serving Him above having a relationship with Him. It's the relationship that He desires. He wants us to know Him. Really know Him, not rules and a way to live, but He longs for us to have an intimate and personal relationship with Him. And He wants us to reveal ourselves to Him. Completely. Honestly. Openly. He wants us to tell Him about our bad days and our good days. Not only will He weep with us, but He collects our tears in a bottle—they are that precious to Him (see Psalm 56:8). He also rejoices with us. And over us (see Zephaniah 3:17). He gets so excited about us that He breaks out into song!

More than that, He desires for us to know His heart. To know Him in as intimate a way as human beings can know God. He reveals Himself through His Word, through our prayer times, through nature, music, friends—anything He can possibly use to reveal Himself.

Unlike earthly friends, He will never let us down or betray us. He will never judge us or condemn us. He will always see the best in us and dream dreams for us that are full of hope (see Jeremiah 29:11). He will always be there for us (see Matthew 28:20). He's never too busy or too far away to listen or care. Many times, He will be there for us before we even ask (see Isaiah 65:24).

Friends with God. It's hard to believe, isn't it? But that's what He calls us. And then He challenges us to be His friends to others, encouraging and sharpening those who love Him and revealing Him and His love, grace, and salvation to those who don't know Him personally. It's a mighty task. But He will equip, enable, and empower us to do it.

While being an author, speaker, and communications director for the Pennsylvania Conference of Seventh-day Adventists, Tamyra Horst enjoys her roles as wife, mom, and friend best.

CHAPTER
6

Where the Closet Meets the Boardroom

Jennifer Jill Schwirzer

My mother often speaks of a retired but still spellbinding local preacher named Richard Mann. She holds him in high esteem, and he is a gifted communicator. On one occasion Mother spoke of Reverend Mann as belittling the act of praying in public. "I used to say grace in *restaurants,*" he said, "but then I realized I was just trying to look pious."

It was funny my mom should mention that. I had recently been in a restaurant and had seen some non-Christian friends. I sat with them to eat, and when my food was served, I failed to pray as was my custom. For days afterwards my conscience pummeled me into analyzing my motives down to the atomic level. Finally, repentance gave me clear enough eyes to see what had been going on in my heart at the moment of compromise.

It was not that I was too *proud* of my religion, but rather that I was *ashamed* of it. This was partly because of how Christianity had been grossly misrepresented, partly because it was unpopular and I didn't want to be unpopular. Fortunately, God has since given me many chances to share my faith with these same people, sometimes to the tune of their sarcastic laughter. Like Peter, my human impulse was to deny Christ where He was unloved, but God has given me another chance to stand where I once stumbled.

You may think I have a guilt complex. It's true that the Bible doesn't absolutely command that we pray before meals. The point is not the practice of blessing food; it is the motives of the heart that underlie all actions. Jesus said, "What I tell you in the darkness, speak in the light."[1] Christianity involves bringing the soul's devotion to Christ into public notice. Witnessing is like kissing God in a public place, letting people know of the tie between the believer and the Believed. In the future, I hope to do more kissing in public.

From prima donna to Pauline Bunyan

When my husband, Michael, and I were first married, he knew much more about hard work than I did. Having been blessed with an excess of physical energy, he had toiled at everything from road building to construction. In contrast, I was a prima donna who had rarely broken a sweat. In addition, I had a mild case of anorexia and relished the sense of waifish frailty that came from being underweight.

All of that ended one summer in Libby, Montana. Mike had a job planting trees for the US Forest Service. We would head to Libby in our travel-trailer home and live on the mountain for the month with two other families, also in trailers. We would cook over a fire, wash clothes in the creek, and spend the days hurling a hoedag[2] into the ground. Actually, planting the trees was Michael's job, but I did everything else, including climbing the mountains with backpacks full of seedlings on my boney little back.

Somehow the hard work cured me of my eating disorder. Sunlight provided a natural mood elevator and blood sugar regulator. The negative ions in the fresh air oxygenated my brain and helped me think more clearly. Muscular exertion improved my circulation and made my heart and lungs work more efficiently. Sweating purified my blood, and my appetite became keen. A psychological miracle occurred as I started to covet being strong over being thin. I remember gathering huge Rome apples and making applesauce over a fire, and even baking bread by steaming it in juice cans placed in a canning kettle. Making a tangible contribution to others brought a self-respect that cured my addiction to dieting.

I'm sure it helped that I was newly married and in love. All through the healing process, I had an abiding sense that the one who subjected me to hardship did it for my good. Mike could see that with a little work therapy, I would regain strength and sanity. I never felt punished, because the source of the sentence was also a source of love. I would load up my little seedlings, sling the backpack over my shoulders, and make the agonizing, nearly vertical trip to my mountain man, who was swinging his hoedag in the sun. A quick conversation and a kiss later, I would be tripping back down the mountain, singing as I went. We are made for exertion, and when love is motivating our efforts, we are as happy as we can possibly be.

In the same way, it was out of love that God consigned His fallen children to a life of toil. While they had always had employment, the disease of sin made a more aggressive treatment necessary. "By the sweat of your face you shall eat bread,"[3] God said, in tones of disciplinary love. And in the physiological and psychological benefits of labor we can see that "he disciplines us for our good."[4]

True producers

On a short-term mission trip to Honduras, one of our translators was a rather unconventional artistic type named Marteen. I learned that he was a music producer, which was exciting to me, being a singer/songwriter and having released several CDs of my own. I would say, "Maybe we could collaborate on something!" and Marteen would say, in a slightly Bronx-tinged accent, "We'll talk, we'll talk." By the end of the trip he had replied that way so many times that I was convinced he was putting me off.

I wasn't surprised, actually. I realized that the quality and scope of his work was well beyond my ken as I listened to samples of it. I was just a poet with a guitar, and he was a big, fat (not literally), important producer who probably charged more than I could afford, anyway. I decided to leave him alone—until I got home and faced a desperate situation. My own producer, working on my current project, was forced to quit for personal reasons. I knew God wanted the project completed, for it was to be a CD devoted entirely to depicting the closing scenes of Christ's life. God had impressed me deeply with the vision for this recording, and I just had to see it through to completion. I needed another producer, and right away. Had God worked providentially to bring me in contact with Marteen? With some trepidation I called him.

"Uh, Marteen, this is Jennifer. I need a price quote from you on a project," I said.

"I was wondering when you would call me," he said nonchalantly.

A few minutes later Marteen had promised to take the project. He believed in my ministry, he believed in my talent, and he believed in the vision I had for the recording. He would do it for free, "as an offering to the Lord."

Months later I held a master recording that was more elaborate and polished than any I had ever done. Marteen had spent *hours* perfecting the arrangements and creating a beautiful, industry-standard sound. And for free.

When someone loves their craft, perfect workmanship is a pleasure. Even more, the creative effort fueled by a desire to glorify God will bring the most far-reaching results. "Whatever you do, do your work heartily, as for the Lord rather than for men."[5] This is productivity of the most lasting kind. The time-serving, paycheck-hungry drones may squeak by with the minimum requirement, but someone who creates as God creates—submerged in the joy of creating and glorifying the Creator—will produce a final product worthy of the passion with which they worked.

Acquiring Bean Curd

An honest business deal is a refreshing experience. Such was the acquiring of "Bean Curd," our 1986 Saab. Needing to replace a failing vehicle, we discussed what our options were. Having spent thousands on car repairs the previous year, we had little left to purchase a new one. It would have to be used, and it would have to be cheap. The problem was, finding a good, cheap used car took time, and time was in as short supply as money.

Rarely do Santa-Claus-type prayers escape my lips, but this time one did. I prayed, "Dear God, I need a car, but I have no time and little money. Please, find one for me. Amen." My prayer was as sincere as it was brief.

The next morning my husband, not even knowing what I had prayed, rose zombielike from sleep and went straight to his computer, typing in <www.cars.com>. In a flash his eyes fell on the magic letters "S-A-A-B," which sent his fingers scampering to the phone. He was on the trail of the very kind of vehicle we wanted. The Swedish makes are known for longevity and so make excellent second-hand cars.

By that evening we were searching out the Saab-owner's residence. The whole affair was a used-car buyer's dream. The house was immaculate; the people were clean-cut, honest types. They had bought their college-aged daughter a new car because her GPA had earned it and now had no need for the Saab. Yet it was with woeful tones that they spoke of selling her. Memories were embedded in every fiber of her carpet. Mom had owned her, and then gave her to the daughter to drive to college. Daughter had tenderly cherished her first car, as the nearly flawless seats and newly installed CD player attested.

On the test drive, the father revealed the trusty Saab's one flaw. "She'll overheat in traffic, if you're not careful. The trick is to turn on the AC. The extra fan cools the engine right off." He demonstrated with a flip of a switch.

And so it was that we acquired our own daughter's first car, which she soon dubbed Bean Curd (as in tofu). Bean Curd is an ugly brownish-red and can chug only about 30 mph up a steep hill. She's more than fifteen years old, and she has 164,000 miles on her as I write this. But in a day when flash and fad dazzle consumers into doling out thousands for increasingly defective merchandise, it was a joy to acquire—for a mere $750—a reliable, frumpy vehicle.

The Saab owners got thirty calls after we drove away with the car. They could have charged five times what they did, but they didn't need the money.

I am determined to observe scrupulous rules of integrity in all my business dealings. My goal is to be fair in everything I do. I want God to say of me, "He swears to his own hurt, and does not change."[6]

Ruling in the fear of God

When I was a younger woman, one of my job situations featured a very unscrupulous boss. While the man was hugely charismatic and talented, his morals were atrocious. As one young co-worker after another fell prey to his seductive charms, I felt the pressure to cater to his swollen male ego. When I resisted his advances, he turned on me like a hissing viper and made my work life miserable.

In desperation, I called the chairman of the board of the organization that governed the business. Spilling out the details of the harassment I was experiencing, I fully expected sympathy and protection. It was not to be. The chairman rebuked me for finding fault with my boss and admonished me to take stock of my own faults and weaknesses. Knowing I was anything but a perfect Christian, I retreated in shame.

Gradually, the boss's tainted principles began to irk the other employees. Over the course of a few years, he lost his best workers and was left with a handful of enablers, shortly after which the business folded. By then I was long gone.

The boss's behavior didn't perplex me so much as that of the board of directors. Why didn't they take control of a disastrous situation and replace the boss with someone who was morally fit to lead? Years later I learned that it was because at least some of them possessed the same weaknesses as the boss.

When we indulge in a moral wrong, we lose the right to correct that wrong in another. This is what Jesus meant when He said to the Pharisees who had brought the woman caught in adultery, "He that is without sin, let him cast the first stone."[7] "Without sin" literally means "without this particular sin," making Jesus' counsel go something like this: "He that is committing adultery is disqualified to punish adultery."

Uncorrected wrongs in the workplace will eat out the heart of any business. Morale descends to dangerous lows when politics and pleasure override principle. David's failure to correct grievous wrong in His kingdom led to widespread discontent and paved the way for Absalom's revolt.[8] In reflecting upon the lessons learned through trial and error, the dying David said, "He who rules over men righteously, who rules in the fear of God, is as the light of the morning when the sun rises, a morning without clouds, when the tender grass springs out of the earth, through sunshine after rain."[9]

Wise as a dove, harmless as a serpent?

My first year of managing Expressly Vegetarian Café, a ministry of a church in Philadelphia, was a crash course in employee relations. It was a small business that I could manage myself with one steady worker and a few occasional volunteers. The "steady worker" of my dreams never appeared, though, and in fact I had five "steady work-ers" leave within the first year and a half. By the time Sheila Truman[10] appeared on the scene, I was once burned and twice shy.

The café was located in the basement of the church, and Sheila had called the church asking for financial assistance. The church policy was to give only food and clothes and not money, but the person Sheila spoke to thought I might be able to use her at the café. She walked in one day, essentially proclaiming that she was our new em-ployee.

After so many walk-outs, I had vowed to be very selective in my choice of employees. More than one deserter had been a person I was trying to help. Well, I was done trying to help people, and now I needed to look out for myself and for the business. I had promised myself to hire only stable people with a good work history and to be much more professional and much less naïve in my hiring. As I heard Sheila's story, things just didn't stack up. I decided against hiring her, thinking there was a strong possibility that it would be another disas-ter.

Two weeks later I saw Sheila Truman and her mother at a local pharmacy. With puppy eyes, Sheila told me things were still going terribly. Yet her mom had a cart full of purchases, and it certainly seemed that if anyone should help, it was her mother. Again, I won-dered if there was something behind Sheila's eyes that she wasn't letting on. But I wondered also if I was just a cranky old employer who had grown hardened and suspicious and unwilling to help people who had genuine potential if they were only given a chance.

Because I didn't hire Sheila, I still don't know which of those two was the case. We are told to be "as wise as serpents, and harmless as doves."[11] I had been wise as a dove for a year and a half. Was I now being as harmless as a serpent? I finally arrived at the conclusion that I needed to put my own sanity and the stability of the business first for a while, lest it fold, or I fold, and no one at all be helped.

Balancing compassion toward potential employees with the needs of the business or ministry is a delicate thing. As the story of Paul, Barnabas, and John Mark testifies, godly men will not always see eye to eye on the how-to of dealing with those who might fail us. Barnabas's disposition to overlook John Mark's failure was probably prompted by the fact that he was a relative.[12] It was, however, richly rewarded when "the young man gave himself unreservedly to the Lord and to the work of proclaiming the gospel message in difficult fields."[13] May God give us heaven's eyes to discern when our trust in someone will bear fruit, and when it will only give *them* a chance to take us for a ride.

Winning Gina

Gina[14] was a fifty-something prep cook at the Auburn, Massachusetts, Friendly's restaurant, and she didn't like me. That would have been tolerable if I had not been a *waitress* at the Auburn, Massachusetts, Friendly's.

"Bacon burger, rare!" I'd put my order slip on the carousel, trying to catch her eye and insert a "friendly" smile. In response, a cold, steely glare.

It was one of those relationships in which the subtleties of body language and voice tone chilled the space between us tangibly. Occasionally a shouted insult or slammed-down plate would pierce the arctic air and into my sensitive soul. No amount of cooperativeness or compliance warmed or softened the enmity, nor did it have a reasonable cause.

I would beseech co-workers to explain, "Why does she hate me?" They would shrug and mutter something about Gina's intolerance of new waitresses. It almost seemed that my willing spirit goaded her on to more meanness. With each renewed effort on my part to remove offense, she became more offended.

One day I stood back from the situation and observed Gina's life. She was an attractive but aging redhead who was a little heavier than she wanted to be. Apparently divorced and single, her social life revolved around a group of waitresses at this burger-and-fries restaurant. There was no dream of a professional future, no hope of anything more in life. She probably wouldn't remarry, and even decent, unmarried dates over fifty were a rarity.

The waitresses were, for the most part, under twenty, and Gina could not regard them as comrades without making herself seem immature. And so she dubbed them "my ladies," a title they bore with pride but hardly deserved. Gina's ladies weren't fascinating conversationalists. The topics they most often dwelt upon were whose backseat they ended up in the weekend before and what intoxicants were coursing through their veins when they ended up there.

Somehow it came to my knowledge that Gina's daughter had a new baby. I heard the echo of Jesus' words, "Love your enemies, and pray for those who persecute you in order that you may be sons of your Father who is in heaven; for He causes His sun to rise on the evil and the good, and sends rain on the righteous and the unrighteous."[15]

I decided upon a bold move. I would give Gina some of the beautiful, almost-new baby clothes that my own baby had grown out of. I brought a box to work, and as I was stowing my purse in the basement locker before the shift, I casually said, "Gina, that box over there is for you. It's clothes for your new grandbaby. I don't need them anymore."

To my surprise, she muttered something quite close to, "Thanks."

Miracles are not always sudden and startling. Sometimes they unfold like the tightly wound petals of a rose, in slow, gracious motion. Gina gradually, gently, accepted me. She would shout out my bacon burger orders with respect, not as if I were a stone in her shoe.

She would actually mutter "Hi," as we passed each other for the first time of the day. Then the crowning wonder came. Just before I quit my waitressing job, I was dubbed one of Gina's "ladies." As I finished out my days at Friendly's in Auburn, Massachusetts, I wore that auspicious title with honor, knowing that simply following Jesus' counsel to love my enemies had won it for me.

Jennifer Jill Schwirzer is an author and musician residing in Philadelphia. She's the founder of Michael Ministries and is married with two teenaged daughters.

---

[1] Matthew 10:27, NASB.

[2] A very heavy, pointed hoe used to wedge the earth apart in preparation for planting a seedling.

[3] Genesis 3:19, NASB.

[4] Hebrews 12:10, NASB.

[5] Colossians 3:23, NASB.

[6] Psalm 15:4, NASB.

[7] John 8:7, NASB.

[8] See 2 Samuel 13–15.

[9] 2 Samuel 23:3, 4, NASB.

[10] Not her real name.

[11] Matthew 10:16, KJV.

[12] Ellen G. White, *The Acts of the Apostles,* 166.

[13] Ibid., 170.

[14] Not her real name.

[15] Matthew 5:44, 45, NASB.

CHAPTER
7

A Matter of Authority

Lincoln E. Steed

It happened quite a few years ago, but I remember the events of that particular Sabbath very well. On that day I changed my sermon a few moments before I got up to speak. It was the day my views on church and state intersected my life in a way that stirred my emotions as never before.

It happened a little south of where you likely live—way down south in Australia. As assistant editor at our small publishing house in Victoria, Australia, I was on the preaching "plan" as they called it back then. It meant taking a different church appointment almost every Sabbath.

Usually the pastor was away, either taking his turn on the plan himself or on vacation. But the Sabbath I met this preaching appointment at what was probably the largest church in the conference, I found the pastor there. And I found him already at quite a fever pitch of excitement when I arrived. The reason soon became obvious: The Speaker of the State Parliament was to present an Australian flag to the Pathfinder club.

Now I will admit that my very first reaction to the pastor's enthusiasm was a little biased by my previous analysis of the type of news stories that typically came in for the weekly division paper that it was my job to edit and assemble. I'd noted a very high percentage were church openings and civic events, usually honored by a local dignitary or two. The story often focused on their presence and was accompanied by a photo of the dignitaries with as many of the church leadership as could fit in the lineup. I paid special attention to these photos, because if the names in the caption were misspelled or out of order, it was sure to generate a flurry of letters. For some time it had troubled me that the guests seemed more newsworthy than our spiritual life or what our message is. But I had said little on the matter.

Before the church service, which was to begin with a Pathfinder march-in, I met with the pastor and our honored guest in the vestry. The politician seemed a nice enough fellow, anxious to please and aware that we were part of his constituency. He seemed not to have been told anything at all about Adventists, which was at the very least an opportunity lost. In five minutes I gave him the barest outline before we walked in and sat down in a row behind the pulpit.

We stood at attention as the Pathfinders marched in with their flag and the national flag held high by the honor guard. They marched past us and planted the flags on either side of the pulpit. I think that was about the point I decided to change my sermon.

The politician gave a rather harmless if thoroughly secular speech for about five minutes. Then we prayed, and the pastor rose to the occasion in that prayer in a most startling way. He praised our guest and said that we were first and foremost citizens of our country. I know by that point I was committed and adrenalized!

In the United States we think nothing of the flag flanking the pulpit, but maybe we should think it through more often. Before that Sabbath in Australia, I had lived ten years in the United States, and have been back in the United States for almost two decades since. But I still remember the unsettled feeling I had the first time I saw the flag inside the church, and I still remember the sense that something wasn't right the first time I recited the Pledge of Allegiance in school (it seems the Supreme Court and a Circuit Court have both recognized the impropriety in requiring that of children).

I got up with my notes and began. In those days I was still inclined to have a pretty detailed sermon outline in front of me. But how could I not speak to the issue at hand?

Much of what I said that day derived from a powerful sermon I had read by Charles Spurgeon, a Baptist preacher from the turn of the last century. He had held forth on the fact that we are already citizens of Christ's kingdom. I love the way Paul puts it in Ephesians 2: "At that time ye were without Christ, being aliens from the commonwealth of Israel, and strangers from the covenants of promise, having no hope, and without God in the world." "Now therefore ye are no more strangers and foreigners, but fellow citizens with the saints, and of the household of God" (verses 12 and 19, KJV).

Spurgeon dwelt much on the fact of our present citizenship in God's kingdom and the fact that we are indeed aliens in this world that has not acknowledged God. I had known something of what it was like to be an alien when I came to the United States as a teenager. I carried a green card that even called me an alien. I knew I was bound by all the laws of the land—there were no exceptions for me. In fact, I was under a closer scrutiny. And as people regularly asked questions about Australia, I saw the reality in the fact that I was under some obligation to explain my country correctly, and that people were judging my homeland by my "witness."

The highest loyalty for a Christian must by definition be to Christ and His kingdom, which is already "within you." The highest attainment for someone who's awake to the claims of Jesus is to serve Him, experiencing His Lordship of his or her life, and then to reign with Him in the eternal kingdom of an earth made new. What comparison can be made between this and the earthly aim that many have—some altruistic, some for corrupt self-interest—to serve an earthly kingdom? I remember reminding the congregation that Sabbath that they were the saints of God, in His house. Having chosen His kingdom, they were inestimably more secure than the most successful worldling, whether in politics, business, or any other endeavor. I pointed out the fact that many will sacrifice all—wealth, friends, honor—for success and power in this world. Worldly success must be counted as failure if they have not chosen Jesus.

The flags behind the pulpit are not "an abomination of desolation." They may indeed be an analog to what the Supreme Court, in upholding a separation of church and state but noting various symbols of religiosity in public life, calls Ceremonial Deism. But they can be a sign of wrong priorities if we see them as more than just a nod to the secular, because they should have no dominant call on us. In fact, it is worth remembering that a church is sovereign property—God's.

During the Middle Ages the sanctity of church property became a significant issue—especially as the Reformation gathered force and the usurped prerogatives of the Roman church were challenged. Still it was always understood that a sanctuary was God's property and within it you were apart from the civil power. From Old Testament times those escaping civil wrath could obtain "sanctuary" on God's premises. In medieval England it was the disgrace of King Henry that he allowed his knight to profane that sanctuary and murder Archbishop Thomas Becket in the Canterbury Cathedral. Except for the king's penance, it might have brought down his kingdom. Even in our day, the Sanctuary Movement played on this ancient understanding to shelter illegal immigrants, who were escaping tyranny. And Seventh-day Adventists are most particular in dedicating churches—an act that, apart from providing a devotional occasion, underscores that it is now God's property, and even acknowledged by the state in its tax-exempt status.

After that church service in Australia, I had quite a discussion with the pastor. Eventually we agreed to disagree and later found we agreed on most everything else. He was, after all, a faithful pastor of many years—just a little intoxicated by the nearness of secular power and forgetful of the Omnipotence he served. But part of his counter to my points that day needs to be discussed, as the texts he quoted can easily be used to justify unqualified support of secular authorities.

In his Epistle to the Romans Paul gave an extended call to honor civil authorities. It is worth noting that he prefaces these comments with the most elevated call to holiness and commitment to God possible. He begins that sequence of verses in chapter 12 with these thoughts, which are seminal to the renewal of mind and commitment to God: "I beseech you therefore, brethren, by the mercies of God, that ye present your bodies a living sacrifice, holy, acceptable unto God, which is your reasonable service. And be not conformed to this world: but be ye transformed by the renewing of your mind, that you may prove what is that good, and acceptable, and perfect, will of God" (verses 1 and 2, KJV).

After specifying just how those with this frame of mind will comport themselves, Paul shifts to our relation to civil authorities. It is worth noting the situation of the church to authorities when he wrote this. Rome was the ironlike overlord in Palestine and most of the known world. It was known for its legal code—applied with severity and an admirable consistency. But Rome was cruel, pagan, and in the process of actually deifying its emperors. The local authorities that ruled by allowance of Rome were corrupt, dissolute, and much influenced by the religious authorities. The church leaders also were corrupt and much opposed to this new Christianity. Having conspired to do away with the upstart Jesus, who claimed to be the Messiah, they were now ready to influence the state to squash His followers. Paul knew the dangerous dynamic presented here and tried to work with it: placating the Jewish authorities as much as possible, while emphasizing to the Romans that he was a law-abiding citizen and due the rights that status conferred. Keep all this in mind when reading Romans 13:1-4.

> *Let every soul be subject unto the higher powers. For there is no power but of God: the powers that be are ordained of God. Whosoever therefore resisteth the power, resisteth the ordinance of God: and they that resist shall receive for themselves damnation. For rulers are not a terror to good works, but to evil. Wilt thou then not be afraid of the power? do that which is good, and thou shalt have praise of the same: For he is the minister of God to thee for good. But if thou do that which is evil, be afraid; for he beareth not the sword in vain: for he is the minister of God, a revenger to execute wrath upon him that doeth evil.*

Before we try to further analyze what Paul might be trying to communicate through this rather severe civics lesson, let's go back a bit in time—way back to Babylon and a great and despotic ruler named Nebuchadnezzar. Actually we have lived through a bit of a time warp of late. Modern-day Iraq actually sits at the confluence of the Tigris and Euphrates rivers, and the site of ancient Babylon is only a few miles along the river from Baghdad. And Saddam Hussein, he of the weapons of mass destruction and wholesale killing of his own people, actually saw himself as a latter-day Nebuchadnezzar. He had been rebuilding ancient Babylon for some time before his regime was overthrown.

Daniel and his fellow captives had been introduced to the court of Nebuchadnezzar in Babylon at the height of that world empire—the greatest known till that time. The king was an absolute monarch, megalomaniacal and arrogant. To this ruler the God of heaven gave a dream of world empires right down to our day and the coming eternal kingdom of Christ. God gave him the dream, but he sought the necromancers and wizards for an answer to the riddle it posed. In fact, he even became vague about the dream itself. In a rage at being denied an interpretation, the king threatened the lives of all royal counselors. At that point of extremity Daniel sought the meaning from the Lord. Perhaps God's purpose all along was to reveal the dream to Daniel, and the king's dream was only to set the scene. Certainly the dream and its interpretation recorded in Daniel 2 are central to an overview of end-time prophecy.

"Thou, O king, sawest," proclaimed Daniel after seeing the self-same dream, "and behold a great image. This great image, whose brightness was excellent, stood before thee; and the form thereof was terrible" (verse 31, KJV). No wonder the king's mind had become fixated on the "terrible" dream! Then, after explaining the different elements of the image and their meaning, Daniel made a statement guaranteed to interest the king: "Thou art this head of gold" (verse 38, KJV).

Daniel had witnessed truth of a most prophetic kind to the greatest ruler of his age—and the king was impressed. "Of a truth it is," he said, "that your God is a God of gods, and a Lord of kings, and a revealer of secrets, seeing thou couldst reveal this secret" (verse 47, KJV). It would seem that the king was living up to Paul's admonition to "do what is good, and thou shalt have the praise of the same [the ruler]."

Some time later "the king made an image of gold, whose height was threescore cubits" (Daniel 3:1, KJV). The head of gold wants it all. And "making an image" in biblical parlance is automatically idolatry. But more than "mere" idolatry, and consistent with his later revealed megalomania that led him to an exile of madness, the king then demanded that all assemble before the image and bow down and worship it—clearly a golden representation of himself, *ergo* the state.

Now is an appropriate time in the story to think on what a superficial reading of Paul is often used to support a false view of civil authority.

In the medieval period and even up to the Reformation times, an idea of kingship took root where the ruler was God's vice-regent on earth—it became known as the divine right of kings. It derived simplistically from the idea of a theocracy and the divine ordination of a ruler. It devolved into an even worse state, where the king's edicts were automatically presumed to be from on high and beyond question—except perhaps, famously in the case of the Holy Roman Emperor, who forgot that he was vassal to the Pontiff. This assumption of divine right actually removed the attention from the justness of the laws a ruler administered and made his authority the issue, regardless of how he administered the laws. No wonder this view of civil rule died with the introduction of the Reformation. In England it was formalized when the Puritans and other reforming factions judicially sentenced and executed King Charles in an act that reverberated throughout the civilized world. In the later secular French revolution, the regicide there showed that the concept was outdated in the eyes of all thinking people, even as they moved toward a secular dictatorship that elevated reason to divine status.

On the Plain of Dura, Daniel's three friends assembled with the populace. They heard the call to worship this perversion of faith—this statist deification. They heard the threat of fiery punishment.

They heard the din of worship instruments. And they stood resolute in their disobedience to a state command.

Amazingly the king was ready to give them another chance. Perhaps he knew their relationship to Daniel. Perhaps he hesitated at his own audacity. But his language was direct: "Bow down at the signal or die."

The "three worthies" knew how to respond. They "said to the king, O Nebuchadnezzar, we are not careful to answer thee in this matter." It was a cut-and-dried issue. In a choice between obeying the state or God, it could only be God. "We will not serve thy gods, nor worship the golden image which thou hast set up" (Daniel 3:16, 18, KJV).

In fact, this story alone underscores the only point possible in Paul's good advice. We are, of course, under the very direct control of whatever civil authority exists where we live. The power it exercises is not derived from God but is exercised in the domain contested between God and Satan. And God is working through all human inventions to reveal His will. We are His agents, bonded by our humanity to the secular order but bound by our promised inheritance to the Divine Overlord.

The story "ends" with the amazing appearance of One "like the Son of God" in the fire with the unconsumed three. Nebuchadnezzar is rebuked for his presumption and acknowledges the God of Shadrach, Meshach, and Abednego.

In the ending to this story, we have an even greater conundrum for those who would simplistically apply Paul's words without reference to context. Because the king goes on to reveal a "conversion" akin to the moralistic state religion that prophecy tells us will characterize an end-time coalition that will presume to compel worldwide obedience. "Therefore I make a decree, that every people, nation, and language, which speak any thing amiss against the God of Shadrach, Meshach, and Abednego, shall be cut in pieces, and their houses shall be made into a dunghill" (Daniel 3:29, KJV).

We must beware of falling under the spell of state power that would compel God's laws, just as we must be on our guard against any secular power that would ask us to go beyond good citizenship and give away our loyalty to God in its service.

But we are to be good citizens. Not just in democratic, free societies like the United States of America, but in Communist systems, under a tyrant's rule, under a junta's fist, even within the mayhem of a failed state. We can do that because we are not political, we are spiritual. All that is good and good for other people, we are called to do. We are called to obey any state that requires these things. And if it requires beyond what we can do, we may indeed find ourselves standing rather conspicuously on the plains. We cannot, must not, seek confrontation with the state. It has a legitimate role in ordering society. Its role is not to order the world of the Spirit.

Ellen White wrote,

> We are not required to defy authorities. Our words, whether spoken or written, should be carefully considered, lest we place ourselves on record as uttering that which would make us appear antagonistic to law and order. We are not to say or do anything that would unnecessarily close up our way. We are to go forward in Christ's name, advocating the truths committed to us. If we are forbidden by men to do this work, then we may say, as did the apostles, "Whether it be right in the sight of God to hearken unto you more than God, judge ye. For we cannot but speak the things which we have seen and heard" (*The Acts of the Apostles*, 69).

And that brings us right back to the New Testament era, and the historical context of Paul's practical advice. Paul and the other disciples were not at all antagonistic to authorities, for the same reason that Jesus could be so indifferent to the tax question, so able to turn the coin to Caesar's likeness and connect it to the whole civil economy, and so calm in assuring Pilate that if His kingdom were of this world, His followers would fight for Him. They had no challenge with authority unless it opposed the authority of Heaven.

Early Adventists had the same sort of apolitical stance. The Civil War clearly had a moral component. In fact, I would think it even better answered to a "just war" than the Iraq war. Ellen White on one occasion said that the South was being punished for the great evil of slavery. Yet it was during the Civil War that Adventists came to our historic position on noncombatancy and outright pacifism. "I was shown that God's people, who are His peculiar treasure, cannot engage in this perplexing war, for it is opposed to every principle of their faith" (*Testimonies,* 1:361).

And can Christians participate in the political scene? Many think so, and many clearly make a shipwreck of their faith and advance partisan interests. Still, we know that a faithful Daniel served without compromise. Ellen White once spoke to students at Avondale College and held out, among other possibilities, that they might even work in legislative councils. We surely should not deny the right of Daniels today to enter the lions' den of political action.

So far as those occupied within the church for preaching and teaching the truth are concerned, Ellen White's unambiguous counsel must still apply. "Those teachers in the church or in the school who distinguish themselves by their zeal in politics, should be relieved of their work and responsibilities without delay, for the Lord will not co-operate with them. . . . Every teacher, minister or leader in our ranks who is stirred with a desire to ventilate his opinions on political questions, should be converted by a belief in the truth, or give up his work" (*Fundamentals of Christian Education,* 477). Whew! No wiggle room there.

The issue of whether to vote or not perplexed the early Adventist believers. They recognized the serious responsibility we share in the actions of someone we might vote into office. But it was resolved at a Des Moines, Iowa, camp meeting in 1881 to support the prohibition movement at the ballot box. Ellen White was called to give her advice—it was a twenty-minute yes. Temperance was a topic she called her "favorite." Later she said the issue was so important that members should even vote on Sabbath if it was required!

Clearly, Adventists, like Christians through the ages, could not be indifferent to moral issues. What Christian could keep silent on things like legalized gambling, legalized prostitution, gay "marriage," abortion, and so on? Our vote and voice on these things can impede evil or, if held back, allow it to prosper. "There is a cause for the moral paralysis upon society. Our laws sustain an evil which is sapping their very foundations [the reference was to legalized drinking]. Many deplore the wrongs they know exist, but consider themselves free from all responsibility in the matter. This cannot be. Every individual exerts an influence in society" (*Gospel Workers,* 387).

Ah, the real issue at last. Evangelism. Salt. Representing God's kingdom to a dying world. We are Christ's, bought with the price of His blood. How could we transfer our bond with Him to any earthly fealty? And how can we not give any good law and honest judge our support? We are about changing society, not about reordering it.

Lincoln E. Steed is editor of Liberty *magazine and associate director of Public Affairs and Religious Liberty, North American Division of Seventh-day Adventists.*

CHAPTER
8

Being an Adventist Among Other Christians

Ella M. Rydzewski

I shall always remember the day I flew with the nuns.

My heart pounded as I readied for my first plane trip in several years. The intense fear of flying had originated with my inaugural flight in a private plane commandeered by a show-off young pilot. I vowed then never again to leave the ground. Now I faced an unknown future by leaving California by plane to live on the East Coast, where my husband had taken a new job. After a few days in Philadelphia, I would be on another flight to Europe. Everything was stressing me. Then God worked one of His amazing coincidences that come as a result of desperate prayer.

Sister Ann and I met at a seminar series in Pasadena, California. A nun from a strict order, she now basked in the light of Vatican II changes. "A real breath of air," she called it. Ann had long given up her nun's dress, but the older ladies at her convent continued to wear black robes and white-trimmed habits.

When I expressed my fear of flying to Ann, she mentioned that she and the sisters at the convent would soon be attending a conference in Philadelphia. We discovered we had reservations on the same plane. An incredible coincidence—I would not only be flying with a friend but with more than a dozen nuns.

On the day of the flight, I rode with the nuns to the LA airport. Ann had told them about my phobia. They prayed for me and surrounded me like an angelic army as we boarded the plane. Ann, at thirty-something, was the youngest of the group, with some of the nuns being quite elderly. I remember Sister Mary in particular. Her wrinkled face shone with the love of Jesus as she took my arm and guided me to the plane's entrance.

Ann sat next to me, but not long after we took to the air, Sister Mary called over one of the attendants and told her about my fear. The attendant disappeared into the captain's cabin and soon returned to tell me one of the attendants had called in sick; and wouldn't I like to take her place? "You'll forget your fear, I promise," she said. I spent the five-hour trip going up and down the aisles, waiting on passengers, and never once became frightened. God answered our united prayers.

In my memory I can still feel the calming presence of the nuns and see their glowing faces. They became my sisters that day. As Seventh-day Adventists we belong to a big family made up of many ethnicities, practices, traditions, and histories. But there is One who bonds us all together, and that is Jesus Christ our Lord. That is why we are all called Christians.

As children of God, we come into a relationship of equals with other Christians. I once read that when we talk with Jesus in heaven, we will find that we didn't know as much as we thought we did. Our knowledge is partial, and no faith has all the truth (lowercase "t") about God. Yet all who recognize Christ as Savior have the Truth (capital "T"). When we finally come face to face with Jesus, we will have no perceived "edge" on other Christians. What we do have is information that, if seen as a frame around a picture, directs us to the picture—Christ. All our information or doctrine must glorify God in Christ. We don't want to emphasize the frame and distract from the picture. He should be first in any contact with other Christians.

Who are Christians?

The name *Christian* covers not only different denominations but a whole range of beliefs about Jesus Christ. Understanding the religious background of another Christian helps us in relating to him or her. Among Protestants we find liberal, conservative, mainstream, evangelical, and some other labels. Denominational labels don't mean as much as they used to, and often we find all these under one label. Conservative evangelicals are most like Adventists in their beliefs about Jesus and salvation through Him alone.

My most in-depth relationship with evangelicals occurred at World Vision International headquarters, then located in Monrovia, California. Working as assistant to the director of the child sponsorship department of this well-known relief agency, I felt fully accepted by my colleagues. The director talked to me often about my beliefs and allowed me to write devotional materials used in manuals. He was a Methodist minister, and I related to him as I would anyone in my own church. As a result of his influence, the organization began supporting a few Adventist schools and orphanages.

We enjoyed daily worship together in our departments. In one series we read from *Steps to Christ,* showing the wide appeal of this volume. I came to know the other workers well, and knowing is how we discover we are all part of the family of Christ.

There are liberal Christians who may not emphasize their belief in Christ as Savior, born of a virgin, and coming again. They tend to have more liberal lifestyles and focus on social issues.

I once worked as a secretary at a "liberal" church in California. During those days many of the members opposed the Vietnam War and took part in peace rallies. My boss, the associate pastor, considered Adventists rigid. I made a point never to argue religion with him, but as we became friends, he encouraged me to express my opinions. I frequently attended midweek meetings and supported their interest in civil rights. I admired their stand on the moral issues in our society, and this influenced my own spiritual journey.

In conversation one day I discovered that the senior pastor erroneously believed and taught that Adventists were Arians. I was able to present him with resource material to counteract this and other mistaken ideas.

Some Christians come from the ancient Orthodox religions. These faiths may seem as dusty as old cathedrals. But differences disappear as you get to know them. For two years I corresponded with Methodius, an Orthodox priest in a monastery in the Northwest. I became acquainted with him through my work at *Ministry*, the Adventist magazine for clergy that goes to non-Adventist pastors every other month. He wrote about his work as a retreat director and the history of the Orthodox faiths. I hadn't realized there were so many of them. He told of his personal faith and relationship with Christ. Later he expressed his sadness when he left the monastery to care for his elderly parents. I read his letters to our General Conference prayer circle. He sent greetings to them and considered himself a part of the group. What I appreciate about the Orthodox churches (as well as Catholic churches), is their practice of spiritual disciplines and the use of retreats.

Roman Catholicism's religious system existed parallel to the Orthodox system. Keep in mind there are other Catholic churches besides the Roman one. As a boy my husband attended a Greek Catholic church. Such churches are not part of the papal system.

Because of the Roman Catholic Church's history of persecution, we tend to be suspicious of that denomination. It is important to understand that when we talk about other religions in a negative sense, we are not talking about members or even clergy; we are talking about a system. Usually these systems are hoary with age and soiled by centuries of prejudices and superstitions. The entropic principle that everything runs down is also true of religions. Individual members deserve our respect. Catholics have also faced persecution at times, even in the early history of the United States.

Even though Roman Catholic history seems ghastly, some of its practices unbiblical, and it still plays politics, as one Catholic lady told me, "If your religion had been around for almost 2,000 years, you would have a lot of skeletons in the closet as well." I think she is right, because the Christian church had hardly developed when its antichrist activities began. Nevertheless, when most secular people talk about "the church" you know what church they are referring to.

We tend to look at Luther and the Reformers more kindly. But they took ideas from their mother church, especially prejudices (Luther's hostility against the Jewish people is well-known). Calvin and Zwingli caused the martyrdom of Anabaptists. Both Catholics and Protestants persecuted Anabaptists.

When a church becomes fossilized and unproductive, the Holy Spirit starts a revival that often leads into a whole new movement, because the old church feels threatened by its enthusiasm. The apostles did not want to start a new religion; they just wanted to renew Judaism with belief in the Messiah. For many years Christians remained a branch of Judaism, until they became separated from their roots and afraid of the state.

So why bring out all of this? For the reason that if we don't respect the religions of others, history can repeat itself in our human hearts just as it did in the medieval church.

In other Christian churches God has those who follow and love Him, even though some may even talk to Mary. They have a heart religion. They seek God and reflect His love within their familiar group. I have known such people.

My first job at age nineteen was as a secretary to Mr. Foley, a Roman Catholic. Together we were responsible for licensing physicians in the District of Columbia. Close to retirement, Mr. Foley had white hair, a sense of humor, and a deep caring for people. He was known as an honest man who wasn't tempted by the physicians who tried to bribe him so they could get quick licenses. He talked of his faith and God with reverence. He and his family wrote to me long after I returned to college.

Acceptance is a key component in relating to other Christians—the ability to feel toward them as you would an Adventist brother or sister, even when they seem more like cousins.

Behavior as Christian witness

They will know we are Christ's disciples by our love, says John (John 13:35). We hear this a lot in the church lately, and I think it's by divine intent. God instills love in us through the Holy Spirit as we ask for it daily. The fruits of the Spirit (see Galatians 5:22) not only reflect what our God is like, but our behavior determines how our religion will be perceived by others. God wants Christians to be transparent, show respect, and treat everyone with kindness.

An area where some fail, yet is so important to non-Adventists, is how we do business. Yes, that also means how we relate to money:

making it, spending it, saving it, and giving it away. How people handle finances doesn't mean that they are necessarily clever investors, but it tells what they value and how much. In a society where so many exchange their reputations for money, Adventists must be above reproach.

Today we hear about being "authentic." Probably the worst term a believer can use to describe a Christian is that he or she is a hypocrite, and it's the same with Adventists and other Christians. We expect people to reasonably live what they say they believe. Being authentic also means admitting our faults and failings when appropriate. That's why confession is healthy. People like people they can relate to—people who understand life's struggles and sometimes fail. How we cope with life's trials speaks volumes about our faith.

Discussing religion

Sometimes Seventh-day Adventism gets misrepresented in the Christian world. The reasons may include ignorance, stereotyping, misunderstanding, prejudice, or even bad experiences with members. But how do we challenge the errors?

Our religion is a sacred subject that should be discussed only when others encourage it. Or, as Jesus said, you might be "[throwing] your pearls before swine" (Matthew 7:6, RSV). There are reasons etiquette tells us to avoid talking politics and religion. Religious discussion can become argumentative if done in an aggressive manner. It also makes some uncomfortable, especially if the initiators are so zealous they attempt to convert everyone who crosses their path. To other Christians this says "you are not saved," and "I've come to save you." Some religions turn evangelism into a work on the path to heaven by giving points for "saving souls." Such motives are self-serving.

Religion is closely tied to one's identity. Imagine how you would feel if someone negated, even by inference, your religious beliefs. So unless one is part of a Bible study, open to all viewpoints, it's unwise to address controversial doctrines unless asked.

Jesus spoke to the common people in parables. He did not overwhelm them by going beyond their understanding. He used everyday examples rather than theological treatises. The words He used and the ideas He expounded depended on His audience. He focused on relationships—between people and between God and people.

Be sure of your salvation. An elderly Adventist pastor told me not long ago how grieved he was to hear Adventists say things like "I hope I am saved" or "If I am lucky enough." "Luck has nothing to do with it," he said, and I agree. Too many of us remain unsure of our salvation, and other Christians will sense this lack of trust.

Terminology plays an important role in communicating with other Christians as well as non-Christians. Avoid Adventist clichés and terms. To Christians the real Truth (large "T") is Christ. We have traditionally called our doctrines "the truth." We aren't using the term properly in this context. There is the truth (small "t") of the Sabbath or truth of some other doctrine, as it is based in Jesus, but never "the truth." Watch for other colloquialisms as well.

One of them is our use of Ellen White quotes. Pastors who frequently quote Ellen White in their sermons need to be aware of how this sounds to nonbelievers who might be present.

Some Christians charge that Adventists treat these writings as equal to the Bible. We know that they are not, and must be careful not to leave that impression. However, many Spirit of Prophecy books do have excellent devotional and biblical material to share with other Christians. When the time is right, we can share belief in recent prophecy. The timing depends on the work of the Holy Spirit and the openness of the other person.

On the family and social level

How much do you say about your faith when working or living with other Christians? That depends on the relationship. Is it casual, a close friendship, a beginning friendship, or in a family situation? How much time do you spend together?

We have already discussed the importance of behavior. It's vital in a family situation. Prayer warrior Robert Morneau once said that some parents talk and even argue about religion with their children so much that the kids suffer religious indigestion. When they leave they want nothing of it. Think how you would feel if someone in your household constantly tried to change you. While respecting the lives of others, we need to keep boundaries around our own time for worship, study, Sabbath, and church attendance.

Religion is not always the same thing as spirituality. When walking in the Spirit, Adventists need to be present with family and friends and willing to talk about issues of the heart—to listen and care intensely. We become comforters, nurturers, and servants. Whenever there is a chance, be helpful, especially at times of crises.

When you make new Christian acquaintances at work or in a social situation and discover what type of Christian they are, you will know better how to relate to them. If they are zealous, born-again Christians, rejoice with them and share your own Christian experience.

On occasion we can become partners with other Christians in drawing non-Christians to know Jesus. As pastors and members become part of the community and work within it, they make friends.

Knowledge about Christianity is increasing. The barnacles of tradition are falling away from the rusty hull of history. The time will come when Bible truth for this age becomes clear. Some already is. A recent documentary on cable T.V. detailed the history of Christianity and how Constantine sent it in the wrong direction. Some scholars are discovering the rationale of doctrines such as death as sleep. They may never wear Adventist labels, but they spread biblical truth. Interest in the Sabbath may soon move from one day in seven to the seventh day. If in our pride we think God's remnant must wear our label, we will be in for some surprises.

Other Christians are writing about and teaching health principles more than ever before in their history. Vegetarianism has become popular, along with the emphasis on health. Healthful living is often the "opening wedge" that introduces Adventism to the public in a positive way. The topic also opens doors for working together in a community.

Close friendships

Long ago I discovered one can build closer relationships with other Christian friends than with cultural or nominal Adventists.

When two people enjoy a talking relationship with Jesus, they have good rapport. This creates a trusting atmosphere in which to discuss differences. Spiritual friends exchange testimonies, inspirational experiences, and reading material. They listen to each others' views without arguing. Guard against arguing about religion—it's a devilish tool to cause division and tension among friends.

Attend other Christian churches with friends and family and invite them to your church. My supervisor at World Vision was one of those rare people who took an interest in others' beliefs, and he gladly accepted an invitation to talk in an Adventist church in southern California.

Occasionally I hear of an Adventist who doesn't think we should attend other churches, because they fear we might be deceived and drawn in by their beliefs. Perhaps these people need more confidence that what they have learned is true. Listening to others often helps us clarify what we believe, and we can often learn spiritual truths from them. If we are afraid of other ideas, perhaps we need to analyze ourselves, and know our weaknesses, prejudices, and disappointments.

Former Adventists in other churches

Disappointment in their church family is the major reason members stop coming. This is not only among Adventists. All of us have been disappointed by people, and even the best of us can disappoint others. But what makes some people more prone to abandon ship? It may be that they have not acknowledged their limitations and weaknesses. They tend to live by their feelings rather than be objective about events in their lives. The person who stays can forget self and look at things from the viewpoint of others, even their enemies. This frees them to pinpoint misunderstandings. Some former Adventists have gone to other churches. After attending these churches, they may become convinced of new doctrines, because they are constantly exposed to them. They also notice the pleasant acceptance of other Christians.

And that brings us to another category of Christians—those with an Adventist background who have left their former church. I met Joan while working at World Vision, and in time she told me she had once been an Adventist. She had joined while her husband was in the military. He came back devastated by his war experience but found support in his church. Her change would unsettle his life even more. Joan felt it her duty to return to his church with him. Soon after I met her, another woman in the department became ill with terminal cancer. Joan cared for this single woman every day after work before going to her own home. Joan revealed Christ in her life no matter what label she wore. I did not try to persuade her to return. I could only say she would be welcome.

The wheat still grows with the tares in all Christian churches.

Now if we are no better than other Christians, one may ask what sets us apart. That is better addressed in other places, but the Adventist Church has the potential to apply its unique beliefs to magnify our Lord and Savior in a more brilliant light than has ever been done on earth. This will not be only because our religious knowledge has increased (it has), but because we long for the Holy Spirit and love Jesus and the people He died for. The time will come when God's people will become starkly set apart from the rest of the world. However, what that group will be called, we don't know. Perhaps they will be called "mere Christians." The days before Christ's coming will be a time of chaos. Certainly the logistics involved would be a barrier to having every believer join one particular organization. In those days human beings will be divided into two groups—those who will trust God and His ways, and those who will seek to survive and take care of themselves at all costs. A fair and just God will provide loving and caring people everywhere the opportunity to choose the Truth as it is in Jesus, and they will.

For now we have no reason to treat other Christians differently from the way we treat Adventist Christians (except being sensitive to their beliefs). Neither nicer (because we want to convert them) or coldly because they don't "have the truth." We should be ourselves—authentic Christians.

Ella M. Rydzewski is the editorial assistant at Adventist Review *in Silver Spring, Maryland.*

CHAPTER
9

Relating to Non-Christians

Jon L. Dybdahl

Twenty-five years ago, most Americans had to cross national boundaries or oceans to seriously encounter other religions. All that has changed. Non-Christian religions are a presence in most towns and all cities of our country. In the United States right now, "there are more Muslims than Presbyterians, more Buddhists than Assembly of God members, and about as many Hindus as Episcopalians."[1]

This change is becoming more and more noticed in the media and in people's lives, but few recognize the many implications it has. Some of these implications are positive. Adventists and Jews will no longer be the only ones who are concerned about pork and other pig products. The differences that some groups like Adventists and Mormons feel in relationship to mainstream society will seem much less challenging in the face of the radically varying doctrines of Muslims, Buddhists, Sikhs, and Hindus. On the other hand, the Bible will not be assumed to be the arbiter of theological discussions. Long-honed arguments for Adventism based on winning other Christians cease to have meaning. We will need to rethink theology and mission in the light of the Koran, the Bhagavad-Gita, and other sacred writings.

In the light of this new situation, how should we relate? In the chapter that follows, I will attempt to answer three basic questions. First, how do we treat our new non-Christian neighbors? Second, what are we to think and believe about them? Third, how might we share our faith with them in a meaningful way?

Showing love

The most basic Christian response to others should be love, since the Bible tells us to love even our enemies (see Matthew 5:44). Certainly the immigrant Hindus next door who most likely want to be friends deserve love. What does love mean in this situation?

A good place to start is a willingness to not prejudge and to seriously listen. *Muslim* and *terrorist* are not synonymous. Neither are *Hindu* and *polytheist*. Just as we are offended when people accept half-truths or popular gossip as truth about our beliefs, we must be careful not to do the same to others. The only way to avoid this is to let them explain their beliefs to us. The place to begin is really listening to them. We must listen respectfully, not prejudging based on popular stereotypes.

In years of teaching world religions to mainly Christian students, I noticed a basic problem. There was a prevailing attitude that was most often not expressed, but that clearly governed all the students' thoughts about other religions. Students believed these other religions didn't make sense. They were either primitive or lacking in rational thinking. People who really thought clearly would not be followers of these religions.

One of my main goals was to help people abandon that viewpoint. First of all, it is not true. One of the reasons these religions have endured is that to their followers they do make sense. Logic is related to culture. To think otherwise is not to love, for love takes the other seriously. Not only is this attitude of ignorance and/or irrationality false and unloving, it opens its holders up to real shock when they encounter a bright, articulate exponent of Islam or Hinduism.

In short, as Christians we are asked by God to love them—love them by listening, taking them seriously, and treating them as we would like to be treated.

A related question that is more challenging to answer is, "What can we do of a religious nature with them?" Can we attend their services? Can our children go to the mosque or the local Buddhist temple with our non-Christian friends? Can we attend a Hindu festival with our neighbors? If we fail to go with them, can we expect them to accept our invitation to church?

The extremes are probably fairly easy to deal with. A public lecture explaining Islam would most likely not be a problem. Participating in a New Age meditation retreat would be off-limits. The vast middle area between these two extremes may be hard to deal with. I suggest several principles.

Principle #1.—Going to learn facts about another religion is not wrong. To gather information about another faith should not be a challenge and even could be part of a plan to share more intelligently our own faith.

Principle #2.—Observing others at worship is generally acceptable. To visit a temple to watch others worship is in most cases OK. As an academy student, I remember visiting the Hindu ceremony of Thaipusam. Visiting a mosque or a Buddhist temple and observing worship is in most cases not a problem.

Principle #3.—Participating in worship is questionable. An exception could be a synagogue visit. Some visitors who went to the Thaipusam ceremony I mentioned above went so far as to have the Hindu sacred yellow mark placed on their foreheads. Such acts seem to suggest mixed allegiance and open one to misunderstanding and to supernatural powers that may be present at such times. Worship participation should take place only when one can explain clearly why in this specific case it is a valid practice. In particular, we need to be careful about sending children unattended to services.

In dealing on a personal level with neighbors and friends, we need to have clear principles in our own minds so we can tactfully and lovingly deal with invitations.

Demonic, or path to God?

The second major issue we face in relationships to other religions is how we think or believe about them. One such question is, Are they demonic and satanically inspired, or are all religions different paths to the same God? Most would agree that neither of these two extremes is the answer. People within various religions can be evil and demon-inspired, but in general it can also be argued that all major religions help to shape society in a good way and combat anarchy and lawlessness. Religions may have demonic elements as well as good elements.

On the other hand, conservative Christians take seriously the words of Scripture found in Acts 4:12, which speaks concerning Jesus, "There is salvation in no one else, for there is no other name given among men by which we must be saved" (RSV). Such words make Jesus special. While not denying some truth in other religions, salvation is found only in Jesus. This rules out, it seems, putting all religions on an equal footing, at least as far as salvation is concerned.

The truth, then, seems to be somewhere in the middle. All religions are not equal pathways to the same place, but neither are they completely demonic. Particularly the high form of these religions does seem to have benefited society in some ways while at the same time containing elements of error and, in some forms, demonic manifestations. Christians do well to remember that the name of Christ does not exempt some Christians and even strains of Christianity from demonstrating demonic behavior. One need only meditate on "Christian" behavior in Ireland and Rwanda to see the truth of this idea.

Saved or unsaved?

An important traditional question usually asked in any discussion of non-Christian religions is, What is the fate of those who have had no opportunity to hear about Jesus? Are they saved or lost? This basic question often leads to others, such as the reason or need for missionaries and evangelism.[2]

While there are many different answers to this question, Christian theologians usually fall into four different camps. On the one side are the *restrictivists*. Their view holds that all the unevangelized are damned. Unless people hear the message of Jesus and respond, they have no hope. This has been the most widely held belief through Christian history, and many present-day evangelical Christians continue to believe and preach it.

Restrictivists find support for their practice in passages like John 3:36: "He who believes in the Son has eternal life; he who does not obey the Son shall not see life, but the wrath of God rests upon him" (RSV). They also find their view gives a powerful reason and motivation for evangelism.

On the other side of the spectrum from restrictivists are *universalists*. Universalists maintain that all sincere religious seekers will be saved. Most Christian universalists see this salvation taking place through the work or merit of Jesus. While there are many varying explanations of how this occurs, one thing is certain: in the end, all—even those who were once rebellious—will be saved. Universalists love to use texts like Titus 2:11: "For the grace of God has appeared for the salvation of all men" (RSV); and, "I when I am lifted up from the earth, will draw all men to myself" (John 12:32, RSV). The strength of the universalist view is that God is clearly very loving, caring, and long-suffering and cannot bear to see any of His creatures lost.

One of the two views between the extremes of restrictivism and universalism is called *inclusivism*. This view holds that because of what God did through Christ, all sincere religious seekers will be saved. This view—also called the "wider hope"—says that because Jesus is the basis of salvation, He can save true seekers of other religions or no religion at all who may have never found Jesus.

As Bible evidence for their position, inclusivists often utilize texts used by universalists but interpret them differently. They would say that the idea of Jesus as "Savior of all men," refers to giving *accessibility* to salvation rather than the necessity of salvation. Inclusivists believe they can defend both the goodness of God and God's gift of the power of choice.

The fourth view is *universal opportunity*. These believers agree with restrictivists that the way of salvation is a conscious response to the gospel. They disagree with restrictivists, however, in that the message does *not* need to come by human messenger or even during the earthly life of the individual. God has a myriad of ways to reach people both in this life or possibly in some post-death intermediate state.

Those who hold the belief that this happens in an intermediate state use 1 Peter 3:18–4:6. They understand this text to mean that Jesus preaches the gospel to the dead.

How do we evaluate these four views? What should be our response? I suggest several overall observations to guide us.

Sincere Bible-believing Christians are in all four camps. We must resist the temptation to label any who disagree with us as heretical. Proponents of all of these views will give texts they feel support their views. This question, I believe, is not directly spoken to in Scripture, and, for reasons known only to God, answers are not specifically given.

Christians should uphold the centrality, sovereignty, and uniqueness of Jesus. All views must be judged in light of Jesus. Some restrictivists, it seems to me, actually restrict Jesus' power (e.g., He can only save if people are reached by a missionary). Some universalists deny the uniqueness of Jesus and seem to feel salvation can be found apart from Him. In relating to this question, we must continually refer back to Jesus.

Christians must maintain a balance between God's love and justice and the clear command to witness. The Bible repeatedly stresses the love and justice of God as essential to His character. It also urges Christians to do and to share their beliefs about Jesus with others (see Matthew 9:37, 38; 28:16-20; Luke 24:46-49; Romans 10:13-17; Acts 1:8).

On the one hand, I find it hard to put myself fully in any of the four major positions. With the restrictivist, I agree that hearing about Jesus is important and makes a real difference in people's lives. With the universalist, I believe God is loving. In agreement with the inclusivist, I believe that a sincere seeking after God is rewarded. With the universal opportunist, I think God can and does sometimes use miraculous means to save people.

On the other hand, I have disagreements with each view. I disagree with the restrictivists in their seeming limitation of God in reaching people. I cannot accept the universalist belief that in the end, no one can really say No to God. I have problems with inclusivists' motives for mission, although if I had to come down in one camp it would be this one. I see serious theological problems with the universal opportunity viewpoint on point-of-death and post-death "evangelism."

I believe that the usual way God saves people is through human messengers sharing His good news. I also believe that God is fair and loving and not limited by our failure to give the message. He can use special means to touch people. He reads the hearts of people and judges accordingly. Whereas Jesus is always the basis for anyone's salvation, some who have not heard His name may still be saved by Him.

This balanced emphasis appears in the writings of Ellen White. On the one hand, she stresses that people are perishing because of our failure to reach out to them.

> Multitudes perish for want of Christian teaching. Beside our own doors and in foreign lands the heathen are untaught and unsaved. While God has . . . so freely given to us a saving knowledge of His truth, what excuse can we offer for permitting the cries of . . . the untaught and the unsaved to ascend to heaven? (*The Ministry of Healing,* 288).

On the other hand, she clearly points out that some non-Christians will be saved:

> Among the heathen are those who worship God ignorantly, those to whom the light is never brought by human instrumentality, yet they will not perish. Though ignorant of the written law of God, they have heard his voice speaking to them in nature, and have done the things that the law required. Their works are evidence that the Holy Spirit has touched their hearts, and they are recognized as the children of God (*The Desire of Ages,* 638).

Motives for mission
In the light of all this, what can we say about motives for mission? I propose five.

1. People's desperate need.—Jesus found the crowds "harassed and helpless, like sheep without a shepherd" (Matthew 9:36, RSV). That is the reason He gave for sending workers into the harvest. Spiritual, social, familial, and physical needs overwhelm our world today.

2. Jesus commands it.—The Great Commission is a command, not a suggestion. Jesus must have known what He was saying. Even if we don't understand all the reasons, followers of Jesus love to obey His command (see Matthew 28:18-20; Mark 16:15, 16; Luke 24:48, 49; John 20:21; Acts 1:8).

3. God uses Christians in mission to lead people to faith and salvation.—Those sharing the good news are said to have "beautiful feet" (Romans 10:14, 15). People cannot believe unless they hear, and they can only hear if a preacher speaks. We can make an eternal difference in people's lives.

4. Sharing benefits the missionary.—In those gripped by God's grace and love, there is a deep, unstoppable inner desire to share it. We would not be happy if we didn't give the news. Paul said: "Woe is me if I do not preach the gospel" (1 Corinthians 9:16). He would not have been satisfied doing anything else. The growth and joy that come from working for people cannot be measured.

5. The great controversy is not over yet.—Christ and Satan are still locked in battle over the hearts and souls of people. Forces of evil still affect human affairs with terrible consequences. Christians in mission are the shock troops of God's kingdom of light, battling back the dark forces of evil. Recruitment for God's kingdom army is a top priority.

While we may not understand in any particular mission situation exactly why or how God is working, the fact that we are there, telling the good news, puts us in the center of God's plan for us and the world.

How do we share?

This brings us to our third major question. How can we win people of other faiths to Christ? I suggest six principles that can guide us as we seek to win non-Christians to Jesus.[3]

1. Build on similarities.—After teaching world religions for years, I came more and more to realize an interesting fact. In the general world of Christianity, Adventists have often felt very strange. We worshipped on Sabbath, they on Sunday; we had dietary guidelines, they didn't, etc. In comparing Christian and non-Christian religions, Adventists had many more things in common with non-Christians than with other Christians. Jews and Muslims refrain from pork. For Hindus (especially mid- and high-caste ones) and Buddhists, vegetarianism is an ideal. Eastern religions are, at core, noncombatant, as we are, while strict Muslims agree heartily with our moral stand against immodesty and easy sex. In other words, in the world of non-Christian religions, Adventists have bridge-building opportunities that other Christians lack. Such similarities are a wonderful place to start a discussion with non-Christians that can build toward sharing Christ.

2. **Make clear the basics.**—The core of Christianity is God's grace freely given, which forgives us and saves us in spite of our sin. The message of salvation by faith alone is very difficult for most non-Christians to understand. One Bible study, two sermons, or three conversations are rarely enough. In Thailand, a colleague and I spent one whole quarter during Sabbath School lesson time teaching this good news to ex-Buddhists who were already Christians, and the light was only just beginning to dawn at the end of those three months.

Getting the unique Christian message across takes time, careful cultivation, and the miracle of the Holy Spirit. Only when this is truly done can we move on to other things. If this is not understood and practiced in our evangelism, our converts simply swap other religious rules for Adventist rules, and the whole pre-existing, underlying system of salvation by works or merit remains untouched.

3. **Emphasize prayer and the spiritual life.**—Prayer and meditation are generally much more crucial to the life of non-Christians than they are for Western Christians. Non-Christians are often much more interested in the spiritual life of Christians than in the doctrinal beliefs of Christians. Muslims faithfully pray five times a day. Hindus and Buddhists pray several times a day at home altars. These people feel they must touch God. If we fail to show ourselves to be people of devotion and prayer who experience God's presence, our appeal is limited. Rarely will people of another faith refuse a prayer for them. Answered prayer is, for them, a clear evidence of God's

work. If we want to impact non-Christians, our devotional/worship/ prayer life must be up-front, dynamic, real, and attractive.

4. Be sensitive to underlying spiritual issues.—Most Buddhism in Asia, especially in rural Asia, is mixed with animism or belief in spirits. While pure, idealistic Buddhism is scandalized by this, many Buddhist temples in Thailand have spirit houses on their compounds that recognize local spirits. In times of crisis, many Buddhists still seek out spirit help. I can remember visiting the grounds of Chiang Mai University at exam time. The house just in front of it was thronged by students praying and burning candles and incense, seeking help in their time of scholastic need. What is true of Buddhism is true of all major non-Christian religions.

5. Don't forget community.—To win and hold non-Christians, the church must create and maintain a strong sense of community and fellowship. A meal or an afternoon of friendship and conversation is evangelism for a Buddhist youth facing ostracism for a growing interest in Jesus.

A sense of care and community from fellow Christians is not optional for a Muslim or Hindu family facing social rejection for their faith in Christ. Doctrine and truth lose their grip quickly if not accompanied by the warmth of real human companionship and support.

6. Contextualize all elements of the faith that are not supracultural.—The fancy theological term "contextualize" simply means to *adapt*. The truth is not abandoned, but it is adapted to fit the culture of the people with whom we want to communicate. Many simple things make a difference—sitting on the floor rather than on pews; allowing men and women to sit on different sides of the church; using a local language other than English.

Some issues become more challenging—singing to a local tune, chanting, using local musical instruments, shaping a church architecturally like a temple. Such things are more difficult for a cultural outsider to accept and promote.

For Adventists, the biggest challenges come when the questions become theological. Must we change the order of subjects in our typical evangelistic series? Should we preach the state of the dead in the same way? How much must a Buddhist or Hindu understand before being baptized? Easy answers are not always available, but the questions must be asked and discussed and prayed over. Unless they are, we can never say, as Paul does, "To the Jews, I became like a Jew, to win the Jews.... To those not having the law, I became like one not having the law.... so as to win those not having the law" (1 Corinthians 9:20-22, NIV).

Conclusion

The non-Christian challenge to Christianity and to Adventism in all its aspects will increase rather than decrease. In the past, we have worked to some extent with non-Christians, but generally our methods and materials have been largely borrowed from North American sources. The time has come when, for the sake of God and His kingdom, we must become serious. We need to pour sufficient resources and our best minds and workers into this challenge. Adventism is uniquely positioned to reach non-Christians in large numbers, but that will not happen unless we allow God to lay this burden on us and we passionately and intelligently pursue this mission. My prayer is that God will help us begin to do that today.

Dr. Jon Dybdahl is president of Walla Walla College in Washington State.

---

[1] Muck, Terry. *Those Other Religions in Your Neighborhood* (Grand Rapids, Mich.: Zondervan, 1992), 14.

[2] Discussion on the following pages is dependent on "Is There Hope for the Unevangelized?" Jon L. Dybdahl, in *Adventist Mission in the 21st Century*, Dybdahl, Jon L., ed. (Hagerstown, Md.: Review and Herald, 1999).

[3] Main points are taken from "Meeting the Challenge of Buddhism in a Changing World," Jon L. Dybdahl, *Asia Adventist Seminary Studies*, 3:85–87.

CHAPTER
10

The Power of Knowing That You Are Loved

Kent Hansen

Jesus' final journey to the cross had just begun. As the time approached for Him to be taken up,

> *He set His face to go to Jerusalem. And He sent messengers ahead of Him. On their way they entered a village of the Samaritans to make ready for Him; but they did not receive Him, because His face was set toward Jerusalem. When His disciples James and John saw it, they said, "Lord, do you want us to call fire down from heaven and destroy them?" But Jesus turned and rebuked them, and they went on to another village (Luke 9:51-56, NRSV).*

It is tempting, isn't it? Wouldn't it be just, and simple too, if we could incinerate those who treat us with contempt because they don't accept our race, our God, or the direction we are heading? Two thousand years later, along the same roads, in the same villages, men and women are attempting to do just that with C-4 *plastique* explosives strapped to their waists and with rocket fire.

There are other methods to eliminate our opposition—whispers, character assassination, withholding information, lawsuits, and sneak verbal attacks. If eliminating those who disagree with us is our goal, there are many instruments to "Get rid of them! Destroy those who don't see things our way!" We observe the attack on the World Trade Center, the conflicts in Palestine and Northern Ireland, the battle between Hindus, Muslims, Sikhs, and Christians in India and Pakistan, the Communist Chinese' relentless oppression of Tibetan Buddhists and Christians, and the culture wars in the United States. These represent the futile consequences of fallen human nature played out to its end, fueled by self-righteousness.

It gets more personal than that. A woman in a Bible study I led was betrayed by her husband, who verbally and emotionally abused her and brought his mistress to live in their home. She was wracked with anger and pain. One night she asked to talk to me and poured out her distress. I pointed out her choices: leave and divorce him or stick by in prayer and determination to see if things changed, which was a highly unlikely prospect.

"No," she seethed. "I don't want to do either one of those things."

"What do you want then?"

"I want you to make him hurt! I want you to make him pay!" It is a request that I know all too well as an attorney. Fortunately, I have stayed away from the practice of family law, where I have seen few satisfactory answers and outcomes. I refer those cases out to colleagues who frankly have more courage and patience than I do.

"And what then?" I asked her, receiving only sobbing wordlessness in response.

Jesus had just sent out His disciples "to preach the kingdom of God and to heal the sick." He said to them in parting, "If people do not welcome you, shake the dust off your feet as you leave that town, as a testimony against them" (Luke 9:2, 5).

"Tell them about God and heal them. If they don't accept you, move on." Hardly the stuff of fireballs! Jesus moves through persuasion and choice. If God's solution to the rebellion of sin was to vaporize those who reject him, then Jesus had no need to make the appointment in Jerusalem. He made that appointment because His way is to give His life, not take a life. Laying down one's own life in love for another is the way of Christ.

A wise woman once told me, "Never let someone else's anger use your authority." Jesus was not about to let James and John, the temperamental Sons of Thunder, use His authority to wipe out some ill-mannered Samaritans. Consider the consequences if He had "nuked" them. His walk to Jerusalem would have been unimpeded but silent: No blind men calling out for mercy; no Zacchaeus running and climbing the tree in joyful expectation of seeing Jesus; no praising children. They would have cowered in their houses and hidden in the woods rather than face Jesus.

"Repent or die" is a statement of consequence. It is not the choice God offers to each of us. "Come now, let us reason together," says the Lord (Isaiah 1:18). "Indeed, God did not send His Son into the world to condemn the world, but in order that the world might be saved through Him" (John 3:17, NRSV). The apostle Paul asked, "Do you show contempt for the riches of His kindness, tolerance, and patience, not realizing that God's kindness leads you toward repentance?" (Romans 2:4). He told Timothy, "The Lord's servant must not quarrel; instead, he must be kind to everyone, able to teach, not resentful. Those who oppose him he must gently instruct, in the hope that God will grant them repentance leading to the truth" (2 Timothy 2:24-26). Peter made the same point about God's merciful ways: "The Lord is not slow in keeping His promise, as some understand slowness. He is patient with you, not wanting anyone to perish, but everyone to come to repentance" (2 Peter 3:9).

When my two brothers and sister and I used to go out for school or play, my mother would instruct us, "Always remember that your mother was a McGrill." That was a line from a beloved story that she read to us, and we knew what it meant. We were to be kind and courteous and fair with others because that was the heritage and character of our family. Jesus made the same point when He said, "Love your enemies," because it is the right thing to do and not because you expect any payback. It will show you to be "sons of the Most High, because He is kind to the ungrateful and wicked. Be merciful, just as your Father is merciful" (Luke 6:35, 36).

God intends His family to be a "class act" and generous. Unconditional love is to be the calling card of His children.

How we learn to love like this

When Jesus told His followers, "Love your enemies," He wasn't offering up a comforting cliché for wimps and sissies to decoupage on refrigerator magnets or inscribe with a peace symbol on a bumper sticker. Jesus was calling us to a love that is tough on principle and tender on people.

Jesus did not command us to do something in a dangerous, sinful world that He didn't do Himself. He did not request us to confront hostility and evil without equipping and empowering us to do so. In the words of Earl Palmer, "Jesus challenges us to stand our ground in the face of chaos with skill and resources that come from our relationship with the Lord of the sermon [on the Mount] and then to offer those healing resources to others."[1]

The ability to love our enemies and do good to them is a direct result of our accepting the deep and true love that God has for us. Because love is a gift, we must possess it ourselves before we can give it to others. It follows, then, that we will never be able to love others more than we believe that God loves us.

God created us in love and woos us into eternal relationship with Him with promises and acts of love. He gives us a choice whether to accept that love as the truth and power of our life.

Without that choice, any relationship with Him would be based on fear and coercion. It would lack the spontaneous response of joy, tender intimacy, and faithfulness that flows from true love.

God backs up His invitation to us with a pervasive, indestructible love that can survive and blossom over every gulf of distance, each hurt to body and soul, every demonic and human power arrayed against us in brutal attack, the shadows of doubt that we harbor in our mind, and everything that we have done or will do or that has been done or will be done to us in the future, including death. (See Romans 8:28-39; Song of Solomon 8:6, 7).

The apostle John walked with Jesus through His ministry and stood beneath the cross when Jesus, in agony, prayed, "Father, forgive them, for they do not know what they are doing" (Luke 23:34). He pondered what he had seen and heard and what it meant for us. He concluded that God's love through Jesus living in the hearts of believers made it possible for us to love without reservation. John wrote the beleaguered first-century Christians:

Dear friends, let us love one another, for love comes from God. Everyone who loves has been born of God and knows God. Whoever does not love does not know God because God is love. This is how God showed his love among us: he sent his one and only Son into the world that we might live through him. This is love: not that we loved God, but that he loved us and sent his Son as an atoning sacrifice for our sins. Dear friends, since God so loved us, we also ought to love one another, God lives in us and his love is made complete in us.... There is no fear in love. Perfect love drives out fear, because fear has to do with punishment. The one who fears is not made perfect in love. We love because he first loved us (1 John 4:1-12, 18, 19).

By "perfect love," John means a love that makes us complete. Every Christian facing an enemy should ask him- or herself, "Do I know that I am completely loved by God and there is nothing that I can do to make God love me any more and nothing I can do to make Him love me any less? Does my enemy know that he or she is loved in this way?" Answering these questions is essential to loving our enemies for two reasons. First, we can never love unless we know that we are loved, and second, when we don't know or forget that we are loved, we resort to power, perhaps even to verbal or physical violence, to attempt by force what should occur only through grace in the freedom of love.

The power of the Cross rests in the truth that the Creator of the universe would rather die than live for eternity without His beloved children. Do you know this truth in your heart as well as your mind? It's strong enough to carry you beyond betrayal. It's tough enough to permit you the honest vulnerability to strip away carefully arranged appearances and defenses. It's enough to bring you to touch the messes and sores that need to be cleansed, to soothe what is bruised and chafed, to face anger, distrust, and betrayal without fear or condescension, in forgiving, healing touch. It's enough to bring you to serve without self-consciousness, to accept the unacceptable and love the unlovely. All things are possible to the one who believes that he or she is truly loved by God.

My work brings me in contact with men and women whose view of God is a harsh taskmaster who will never be pleased until perfection is attained in this life or whose trust levels have been destroyed by capricious pain from sources where they should have received love. They are often paralyzed in fear and wracked with guilt that they will never be good enough to be loved. They can be frustrated, angry, and even vicious in their hopelessness. Their fear and loathing petrifies their relationships, private and public. My message to them is simple: "The Creator of the universe and the Redeemer of the world loves you not just as a theological principle, but as a personal fact. He learned this love from His Father, who is your Father. His love for you will never end. Therefore you are free to live and love and do what needs to be done." Many times I have had hostile, enraged men and women respond with tears of relief and open hearts when I tell them, "Jesus Christ loves you and has sent me to tell you so."

Putting the truth into practice

There is no way around the fact that loving your enemies is hard work and exacts an expensive toll. It cost Jesus' life, and there is no guarantee that it won't cost ours as well. Read through Luke 6:27-36 and see Jesus' itemized list of the prices of following His lead in this matter. It will cost us pride. We may receive blows, even physical injury, and loss of our property right down to the shirt off our back, and writing off accounts receivable that we expect to fund our lives in comfortable retirement.

We can't avoid that cost by pushing off its reality into abstract hypothetical discussions of ethical responses to conflicts half a world away from us, or asking, "What would you do if a terrorist threatened to blow your child's head off if you didn't help him betray your nation?" When Jesus said "love your enemies," He was making the issue personal and practical. He spoke of the risk of this love in terms of our personal image, well-being, property, and security.

There is an even greater temptation to get the obligation out of the way fast through an exercise of might to make right what we believe to be wrong. This is especially true if we believe we are serving a good cause greater than ourselves that can be advanced through our forceful effort. The late Christian author Henri J. M. Nouwen draws a compelling lesson from history about the error of this approach:

One of the greatest ironies of history of Christianity is that its leaders constantly gave in to the temptation of power—political power, military power, economic power, or moral and spiritual power—even though they continued to speak in the name of Jesus, who did not cling to His divine power but emptied Himself and became as we are. The temptation to consider power an apt instrument for the proclamation of the Gospel is the greatest temptation of all. We keep hearing from others, as well as saying to ourselves, that having power—provided it is used in the service of God and your fellow human being—is a good thing. With this rationalization, crusades took place; inquisitions were organized; Indians were enslaved; positions of great influence were desired; Episcopal palaces, splendid cathedrals, and opulent seminaries were built; and much moral manipulation of conscience was engaged in. Every time we see a major crisis in the history of the Church … we always see that a major cause of rupture is the power exercised by those who claim to be followers of the poor and powerless Jesus.

What makes the temptation of power so seemingly irresistible? Maybe it is that power offers an easy substitute for the hard task of love. It seems easier to be God than to love God, easier to control people than to love people, easier to own life than to love life. Jesus asks, "Do you love me?" We ask, "Can we sit at your right hand and your left hand in your Kingdom?"[2]

It is easier to intimidate people than to persuade them. But that's not freedom of choice, and that is not Jesus' way. He is after an eternal relationship of love, not quick, coerced compliance. Martin Luther noted that "if men are converted because of fear they will later hate their conversion."

If we are strong enough, wealthy enough, or powerful enough, we may make our enemies do what we want them to do. We are powerless, however, to make them love us. This is a point that I have painfully learned as an attorney. Clients come to me and say, "I don't care what it costs. I'd rather spend my money on you to fight than to give it to my adversary. Anyway, it's the principle of the thing that I care about, not the money."

I have to tell them, "Listen to me. Even if we convince a jury to award you one million dollars, it doesn't mean your adversary will concede that you are right or to give you their hearts and minds. I may hurt and embarrass your opponent in court, but I can't win his love for you."

The apostle Paul was no stranger to the law courts, and he knew what I am talking about here. He told the litigious Corinthian believers, "The very fact that you have lawsuits among you means you have been completely defeated already. Why not rather be wronged? Why not rather be cheated? Instead, you yourselves cheat and do wrong, and you do this to your brothers" (1 Corinthians 6:7, 8). Paul said this because if we push our conflicts into court, we are seeking a victory of force, not a solution of love, and we have left the instructions of Jesus behind.

After twenty-four years as an attorney, I am astonished still at the willingness of some Christians to follow their "principles" right into the courtroom regardless of the cost of relationships with brothers and sisters for whom Jesus Christ died. When I try to convince them of the destructive futility of their quest for vindication, the frequent retort is, "You're too soft. Principle costs. I need an attorney who will fight for my rights. I'd rather pay you to fight than give that man [or woman] a dime."

I chuckle ruefully when I'm attacked like this because it proves Paul's point that there is something worse than being wronged, cheated or defrauded, and that is the loss of fellowship. Jesus placed such a premium on our relationships that He said that our forgiveness of those who wrong us is the condition of our forgiveness by our heavenly Father and the key to answered prayer (see Matthew 6:12, 14; Mark 11:22-25). In fact, Jesus taught that reconciliation with those we have wounded in our anger ranks in priority over our worship. "But I tell you that anyone who is angry with his brother will be subject to judgment....Therefore, if you are offering your gift at the altar and there remember that your brother has something against you, leave your gift there in front of the altar. First go and be reconciled to your brother; then come and offer your gift" (Matthew 5:22-24).

Christ loved His enemies so much that He died for them. As if that wasn't enough, Christ loved His enemies so much that He lives to save them (Romans 5:6-11). The blood of Jesus does not distinguish between friends and enemies in its flow. The love of Christ surpasses our knowledge of right and wrong, friend and foe, in its transforming power. If we don't receive this point as our reality then we need to spend more time in prayer to change the perspective of the eyes of our heart "to grasp how wide and long and high and deep is the love of Christ, and to know this love that surpasses knowledge—that you may be filled to the measure of all the fullness of God" (Ephesians 3:18, 19).

I read a story of a French priest who gained this perspective of limitless love transcending national and doctrinal differences in a moment of pain and grief. His response challenges me as a Christian and an Adventist.

In World War II, a group of soldiers was fighting in the rural countryside of France. During an intense battle, one of the American soldiers was killed. His comrades did not want to leave his body on the battlefield and decided to give him a Christian burial. They remembered a church a few miles behind the front lines whose grounds included a small cemetery surrounded by a white fence. After receiving permission to take their friend's body to the cemetery, they set out for the church, arriving just before sunset.

The priest, his bent-over back and frail body betraying his many years, responded to their knocking. His face, deeply wrinkled and tan, was the home of two fierce eyes that flashed with wisdom and passion.

"Our friend was killed in battle," they blurted out, "and we wanted to give him a church burial."

Apparently the priest understood what they were asking, although he spoke in very broken English. "I'm sorry," he said, "but we can bury only those of the same faith here."

Weary after many months of war, the soldiers simply turned to walk away. "But," the old priest called after them, "you can bury him outside the fence."

Cynical and exhausted, the soldiers dug a grave and buried their friend just outside the fence. They finished after nightfall.

The next morning, the entire unit was ordered to move on, and the group raced back to the little church for one final goodbye to their friend. When they arrived, they couldn't find the gravesite. Tired and confused, they knocked on the door of the church. They asked the old priest if he knew where they had buried their friend. "It was dark last night and we were exhausted. We must have been disoriented."

A smile flashed across the old priest's face. After you left last night, I could not sleep, so I went outside early this morning and *I moved the fence.* "[3]

Jesus said, "My Father is still working, and I also am working" (John 5:17, NRSV). Once in a while we are privileged to glimpse the Father and Son at work and to join them in the task—sometimes in a courtroom, on a battlefield, in our family rooms and at our dining-room tables, in our workplaces, and maybe even in our pews.

The places where we live and work and worship are the places where Jesus asks us to love our enemies. This is a sacred calling because it is a continuation of the ultimate love that Jesus demonstrated on the cross. Paul wrote: "[God] has committed to us the message of reconciliation. We are therefore Christ's ambassadors, as though God were making His appeal through us" (2 Corinthians 5:19, 20).

What Paul saw as a job, Jesus described as a family characteristic. "Blessed are the peacemakers for they will be called sons of God" (Matthew 5:9). No one could pay us enough to love our enemies. That's the point Christ was making. Peacemaking makes enemies into family members. Family members don't need to be paid for what they do for each other. Family members help each other out of love.

Kent A. Hansen is an attorney and writer living in Corona, California, where he practices business and healthcare law.

---

[1] Earl Palmer, *The Enormous Exception* (Dallas, Tex.: Word, 1986), 56.

[2] Henri J. M. Nouwen, *In the Name of Jesus* (New York: Crossroad, 1989), 58, 59.

[3] Michael Yaconelli, *Messy Spirituality* (Grand Rapids, Mich.: Zondervan, 2002), 126, 127, quoting from William Barclay, *The Daily Study Bible* (Philadelphia: Westminster, 1954), 135.

CHAPTER
11

Limiting Caesar to What Is Caesar's

James Coffin

American Seventh-day Adventists had their religion put to the test in ways that few may have even recognized when terrorist-hijacked jets slammed into New York's World Trade Center, the Pentagon, and the soil of western Pennsylvania on September 11, 2001.

The general populace of the United States experienced a surge of patriotism unparalleled in recent decades. Flags, signs, and a host of other symbols of patriotic fervor emerged overnight in homes, businesses, government buildings, and churches of all denominations. Rich and poor, radical and reactionary, Democrat and Republican, Catholic and Protestant, atheist and believer—all embraced each other, at least briefly, as the United States tried to catch its collective breath and come to grips with the nature and magnitude of what had happened.

Church attendance the weekend after September 11 equaled or surpassed the inflated levels that are customary at Christmas and Easter. People felt a need for the comfort and security of the church. And church leaders felt a need to put the shocking events into some sort of perspective.

In many congregations that first weekend's worship resembled a patriotic pep rally. It was clearly an "us-against-them" scenario. It was nationalism at its best—or worst, depending on your perspective.

99

The reaction raised interesting and integral questions: How much should the church bear the trappings of nationalism? Does nationalism militate against the church's greater mission? Are the two mutually exclusive?

Let's note some background.

In Old Testament times, heritage was vital. That's why we encounter genealogies so often. Pedigree counted. Your forebears could make or break you. Your *bona fides* was established by your lineage—if you were a Jew, that is. If you weren't a Jew, no lineage could adequately compensate for your "Gentileness."

The mixed-blood Samaritans were despised. The conquering Romans were hated. The heathen (but culturally impressive) Greeks were considered spiritually inferior. In fact, Jews applied the foregoing adjectives—and many more like them—to all Gentile groups. Never mind that human beings don't choose their biological parents, their place of birth, and a host of other life circumstances.

Equally important to the Jews were X and Y chromosomes—at least, what we know today the X and Y represent. Y was in; X was out. Y mattered; X didn't. Females were little more than goods and chattel in Old Testament times. Although Moses substantially improved the lot of women, equality wasn't even hinted at until the New Testament. And even then, to a great degree, in practice it remained just that—a *hint.*

Of course, social and economic status was important back then, too. The lowest on the socioeconomic scale were slaves. Possessing virtually no rights, they were at the mercy of their masters. The very fact that they were slaves, Jews believed, said something about their value in God's eyes.

Gentiles, women, and slaves—all were second-class citizens at best. Thus, in Christ's time, the devout Jewish male began each day with a prayer of thanks that he hadn't been born a Gentile, a woman, or a slave. Being all three would have been a fate so terrible as to defy imagination.

Surprisingly, the apostle Paul declares that these national, ethnic, gender, and socioeconomic delineations were insignificant in the new spiritual community that Christ came to establish: "There is neither

Jew nor Greek, slave nor free, male nor female, for you are all one in Christ Jesus" (Galatians 3:28).

In Colossians 3:10, 11, Paul says our social outlook changes dramatically when we have "put on the new self, which is being renewed in knowledge in the image of its Creator. Here there is no Greek or Jew, circumcised or uncircumcised, barbarian, Scythian, slave or free, but Christ is all, and is in all."

The Message paraphrase of Colossians 3:10, 11 states it even more graphically: "All the old fashions are now obsolete. Words like Jewish and non-Jewish, religious and irreligious, insider and outsider, uncivilized and uncouth, slave and free, mean nothing. From now on everyone is defined by Christ, everyone is included in Christ."

Paul's statement in Galatians, bolstered by its counterpart in Colossians, constitutes one of the most radical social manifestos ever set forth. Yet it's crucial if the gospel is to have impact "in Jerusalem, and in all Judea and Samaria, and to the ends of the earth" (Acts 1:8).

Being part of the body of Christ must take precedence over all other affiliations, whether those affiliations were assets or liabilities in the old system of values. The Christ connection is the ultimate definer. The old national/ethnic, gender, and socioeconomic barriers must be forever dismantled. Moreover, when Paul observed the old barriers being erected once again—even by someone as significant as Peter—he "opposed him to his face" (see Galatians 2:11-13).

The new values demanded of Christ's followers are so foreign to our nature that Jesus described the requisite change as being "born again" (John 3:3). It's like having the slate wiped clean. A new start. A totally different set of parameters. A new default setting. A new worldview. And this new-birth experience doesn't have to do only with one's relationship to God. It entails a new understanding of our obligation to our fellow human beings, as well.

Both Jesus and Paul support civic responsibility. Jesus says to "give to Caesar what is Caesar's" (see Matthew 22:17-21). And Paul admonishes us to submit ourselves to the "governing authorities" (see Romans 13). But we don't derive our prime identity from any earthly affiliation. Not our national or ethnic heritage. Not our gender. Not our socioeconomic status. Our prime identity—and the one next to which all other definers pale into insignificance—comes from our connection to Jesus. Which is why Paul could say so emphatically, "I resolved to know nothing while I was with you except Jesus Christ and him crucified" (1 Corinthians 2:2).

The congregation where I pastor has a philosophy brochure that states, in part:

> Markham Woods Church's goal is to create an overarching spiritual culture and community that incorporates people of different races, different ethnic backgrounds, different socio-economic status, different educational levels, different ages, different personalities and different perspectives.
>
> This is in keeping with the apostle Paul's assertion in Galatians 3:28: "There is neither Jew nor Greek, slave nor free, male nor female, for you are all one in Christ Jesus."
>
> The Bible doesn't deny our group differences or our individual differences. It simply says that the Christ culture transcends all other delineations. We aren't first and foremost Anglo or African American, Hispanic or Asian, rich or poor, educated or uneducated, young or old, male or female, liberal or conservative. These are all secondary to the Christ culture.
>
> The Christ culture is the ultimate definer. The Christ culture is the power that allows us to rise above all barriers. The Christ culture is the bond that allows us to have unity in the absence of uniformity. The Christ culture is all-inclusive and all-encompassing.
>
> The Christ culture focuses on love, forgiveness and acceptance. And, as our church's Statement of Philosophy says, the Christ culture inspires us to want to become all that God has in mind for us to be.

Christianity is about Jesus. Jesus should be the focus of our worship and communal interaction. At a practical level, all spiritual exercises must avoid any activity, ritual, or symbol that re-establishes the national, ethnic, gender, or socioeconomic barriers that Paul decries. Mingling the trappings of Christianity with those of nationalism or tribalism potentially erects barriers—however unintended—between fellow Christians. More dangerous still, it causes Christians to become confused as to the relationship that *should* exist between these differing aspects of life.

Let me cite examples from my own experience. While my observations are based on life in the United States, the foibles I describe are endemic in every nation, tribe, and people. I'm addressing a worldwide phenomenon. And in the same way that it poses a threat to our denomination in the United States, similar actions and attitudes pose an equal threat elsewhere.

A few years ago someone in our congregation suggested that it might be nice to conduct a special church service honoring our veterans, in conjunction with the US holiday we call Veterans' Day. However, as we discussed possibilities, problems emerged. What exactly did we mean when we said "our" veterans? Were we speaking as citizens of a nation or as members of a church? Clearly, we discovered, the two were not synonymous.

The United States is like a large stew pot, with people of every type thrown together. People from throughout the world have settled here permanently. Many others reside here for prolonged periods because of employment or the pursuit of education. So in our congregation, we had four categories of veterans: veterans of the US military, veterans of a US ally, veterans from countries that had fought neither for nor against the United States, and veterans of countries that had been major US enemies. So who should we honor in a *church* celebration of "our" veterans?

If we honored just the veterans of the US military, how would an ally feel who had perhaps been stationed in the same place and who had made the same sacrifices for the same cause? Wasn't that person's contribution equally worthy of recognition? And hadn't it helped the United States?

For that matter, hadn't a veteran of a neither-friend-nor-foe country sacrificed in exactly the same way for the benefit of his or her native land? So what were we honoring? Commitment to one's country and the willingness to do one's civic duty? Or commitment to US interests?

All were equally members of the congregation. So how could the congregation single out some its veterans for honor while excluding others? Was the church first and foremost American? Or first and foremost Christian? What did we really want to honor?

Of course, the real stumbling block was the possibility of including "enemy" veterans. Yet these men and women, when called to serve, had done their civic duty as adjured to do by both Christ and Paul. In fact, some had served in noncombatant positions because of their deep respect for human life. So while they might have been affiliated with the enemy military machine, they were, in fact, committed to minimizing the loss of life—United States, its allies, or any other.

The idea of including these former enemies of the United States in any kind of church-sponsored act of recognition was totally unpalatable to a majority of those in the brainstorming group. In the final analysis, the recognition service had to be a celebration of US nationalism. Anything else was unacceptable.

In the end, we decided to do nothing at all. But at least we wrestled with the issue. Most congregations wouldn't have done even that. They would have just proceeded, oblivious to the subtle-yet-insidious resurrection of the national and ethnic barriers that Paul said must be broken down.

"Is it that big a deal?" some might ask. "After all, we're talking about only a relative handful of people. So does it really matter?"

Yes. It does.

In fact, the fewer there are who seem to be directly affected by this subjugation of Christianity to nationalism or tribalism, the more it may matter. While fewer people will be made to feel like second-class members of their congregation, the congregation is also less likely to ever become aware of what it's actually doing. And what it's doing is deriving its prime identity from an earthly nation rather than from the kingdom of God.

A second example of our ever-present latent nationalism/tribalism can be seen in many of the prayers we offer. At a service I attended in the United States not long after September 11, 2001, the person offering the main prayer asked for God's blessing on President George W. Bush and other US government leaders; our US service personnel and their families; our nation as a whole; and a long list of other US-based entities. Don't misunderstand me: There certainly isn't anything wrong with praying for all of these. More to the point: We *should* pray for them. The problem is the stark absence of certain other entities and the unstated implications inherent in our selection of who and what to pray for.

Suppose that an Afghan or an Iraqi Christian were worshiping with us. Would that worshiper have the sense that he or she was among a group whose prime identity *transcended* national and ethnic boundaries? Or would that person feel that we were merely attaching the name of God to the promotion of our own national interests?

Could our prayers not be less partisan? Could we not pray for wisdom for *all* world leaders instead of just for the President of the United States? Could we not pray that God would give *all* soldiers spiritual solace at a time when their lives are in danger and family and friends are far removed?

Could we not pray for *all* whose lives have been torn apart because loved ones have had to leave family and home to go fight for their country? Could we not pray for *all* who are mourning the death of a relative because we as human beings haven't yet figured out how to settle differences without killing each other? Could we not pray for *all* whose homes and possessions have been destroyed by war, whoever and wherever they may be?

Could we not pray for *all* children who will grow up without a father or mother or brother or sister because of the terrible conflicts that exist in our world? Could we not pray in such a way that *all* listeners would feel affinity not only with Americans but also with the flesh-and-blood, pain-feeling, sorrow-experiencing people who are on the other side of the conflict or in conflicts in which we as Americans are playing no part? Could we not pray for those who, while labeled our "enemies," are likewise pleading with God that, if possible, this cup might pass from them?

I would suggest that unless our prayer can equally apply to a fellow human being from an "enemy" country, it's an inappropriate prayer—whether anyone from that country is physically present in our worship service or not. We need to seriously, humbly, and prayerfully ponder this matter.

We may be justified in talking in nationalistic terms to fellow Americans (or fellow Germans or Kenyans or Indonesians, if we come from those countries) for whom nationhood provides our prime identity. But when we're worshiping with those whose prime identity is derived from their citizenship in the kingdom of God, nationalism and tribalism must fade into oblivion. As individuals, we may be proud of our national and ethnic heritage. But as a Christian community, we must recognize that if our love of our earthly heritage in any way erects a barrier between us and others who make up the body of Christ, we're resurrecting the wall that both Jesus and Paul sought to tear down.

My wife and I have three sons. Because my wife is Australian and I'm American, our children have the privilege of being "dual nationals." They each have two passports. They each are 100 percent American, with all the rights and responsibilities that US citizenship entails. And they each are 100 percent Australian, with all the rights and responsibilities that Australian citizenship entails. Both countries have one restriction, however: They must enter Australia on their Australian passport, and they must enter the United States on their US passport. They must at any given moment claim citizenship in the country (the United States or Australia) on whose turf they are.

I would suggest that each Christian, each Seventh-day Adventist, is a dual national. We are citizens of an earthly kingdom, and we are citizens of the kingdom of God. We have all the rights and responsibilities afforded by both kingdoms. I would further suggest that the church is the embassy of the kingdom of God. While it may be constructed within the realm of an earthly kingdom, it is the turf of the kingdom of God. In all our dealings and interactions while in the embassy of the kingdom of God, we're operating under the passport of that kingdom, and we're expected to honor the values and priorities of that kingdom. Ironically, those values and priorities are radically different from the values and priorities of the United States or any other earthly power.

For example, in the kingdom of God, the leaders should work as servants. The first shall be last, and the last shall be first. We're to love our enemies and do good to those who wrong us. We're to ignore national and ethnic differences. We're to ignore socioeconomic differences. We're to ignore gender differences. In fact, we're to ignore just about every line of demarcation that our relative societies have established. And, while we're to recognize our dual-national status, the values of the kingdom of God must take precedence if the two powers ever come into conflict. The earthly kingdom is to be judged on the basis of the heavenly kingdom, not the other way around. If we're to err by being too loyal one way over another, it must be toward the heavenly.

During my years as an editor, I encountered several stories of repressive regimes who viewed the Seventh-day Adventist Church as an extension of the US Government because of the US flags they saw in pictures (printed in church publications) of American churches. A far better message would be sent by having the flag of every nation in the world displayed in every church—because our mission and message are global, not nationalistic. The presence of such flags would be a constant reminder that all citizens of all countries share equal access to God's grace. Granted the impracticability of including all flags, however, the second-best option is to have none.

As an American, I feel that the United States was founded on lofty principles. I also feel that the United States has encouraged spirituality in an admirable way. Such beliefs make it easy to me, as an American, to assume that God and country are more or less synonymous. But it's a false assumption. God and country are never synonymous. The kingdom of God must always take precedence over the kingdoms of this world—irrespective of how admirable or otherwise those countries may be.

We must remember that the Jews of old also had a country based on lofty principles. The Jews were committed also to far higher principles than were the surrounding nations (though perhaps barbaric by today's standards). Yet God, through Paul, said that their pride in their national and ethnic heritage must be superseded by their connection to Christ. God and country have to be separated.

In the church, Jesus (not the US flag or any other country's) and the Bible (not the US Constitution or any other country's) should be uplifted.

But won't such an emphasis cause our loyalty as citizens to be questioned?

Not if we take our civic responsibilities as seriously as Christ and Paul admonish. Not if we are indeed the "salt of the earth" (Matthew 5:13). Not if we are indeed "a city on a hill" (Matthew 5:14). Not if people indeed see our "good deeds" and as a result glorify our Father in heaven (Matthew 5:16).

It isn't necessary to wear our nationalism on our spiritual shirtsleeves if we give to Caesar what is Caesar's with the same level of commitment that we give to God what is God's. But we must keep the two separate and distinct.

The crucial thing, as Paul states so eloquently, is that we must never lose sight of the fact that for the Christian, all the phony barriers we have erected must be laid waste. We must reach a level of equality that has never before existed. We must ensure that, in the church—the kingdom of God— "there is neither Jew nor Greek, slave nor free, male nor female, for [we] are all one in Christ Jesus" (Galatians 3:28).

James Coffin is senior pastor of the Markham Woods Seventh-day Adventist Church in Longwood, Florida, and director of the General Conference Global Mission's Center for Secular/Postmodern Mission, <http://www.secularpostmodern.org>.

CHAPTER
12

Practical Ways to Support Our Leaders

C. Garland Dulan

The concept of leadership is an idea that dates back to Bible times, when leaders were selected by the Lord to lead His people during various periods of history. In many instances God selected leaders to lead His people back to Him or to make clear the direction He wanted His children to follow.

Today, leaders are selected to assist the church in carrying out its mission. The mission of the Seventh-day Adventist Church is to proclaim the gospel to all peoples, leading them to accept Jesus Christ as their personal Savior and nurturing them in preparation for His soon return.[1] Thus, leadership support should be considered in the context of ways to enhance the expected outcomes of the church's mission. Often we find careful thought is given to the selection process but little attention paid to the follow-up support the leader needs. The issue of support is critical since we would expect that the greater the support for leaders within the church organizational structure, the more positive will be the outcomes to mission.

The spirit of leadership

The call to leadership should not be taken lightly; it is a call to kingdom building—God's kingdom. Leaders such as pastors, teachers, church, community, health, and educational administrators provide a service to the church and its associated institutions. Those elected or selected to positions of leadership should view it as a call to serve others.

Every church member has a ministry, an assignment to perform. The apostle Paul indicates that "there are diversities of gifts, but the same Spirit ... [and] the manifestation of the Spirit is given to every man to profit withal" (1 Corinthians 12:4-7, KJV.) These diverse gifts are distributed and controlled by "the same God which worketh all in all" (verse 6). The gifts of God are distributed so that one is given wisdom, another knowledge, another receives the gift of healing, another is given the gift of prophecy, and so forth (see 1 Corinthians 12:8-10). Leadership, I believe, is also a gift from the same Spirit. The gift to lead neither exceeds nor is diminished by other gifts. Thus, as with other gifts, leadership is not to be associated with a prideful spirit. Pride of position should have no place in God's cause, since we all stand equal at the foot of the cross of Christ.

The purpose of support

Providing effective support to leaders can result in outcomes that are beneficial to the church organization and to the church leaders themselves. Outcomes beneficial to the long-term operation of the church are (1) the retention of skilled leaders; (2) the recruitment of increased numbers of effective leaders for the organization; and (3) the development of skilled leaders. Support for leaders provides (1) greater confidence in the ability to provide effective leadership; (2) increased motivation to work within the church; (3) enhanced feeling of personal connectedness to the church organization; and (4) the acquisition of skills and knowledge that positively impact the leader's performance within the church organization, as well as in other areas of life.[2]

Organizations have the responsibility to provide the quality of support that leaders need to carry out the work they have been called to do. The time and the level of support provided should reflect individual needs. Each leader also has a responsibility for his or her own personal development and should seek help and support when necessary.

Areas of support

There are three areas of support that a leader needs—technical, social, and personal.

Technical support includes resources that provide the leader with the practical skills and information that he or she needs on an ongoing basis to do the job. Technical support can be provided through workshops, seminars, and materials that assist leaders in obtaining information that is relevant to the responsibilities of their specific position. Technical support should be intentionally provided by the church organizational unit.

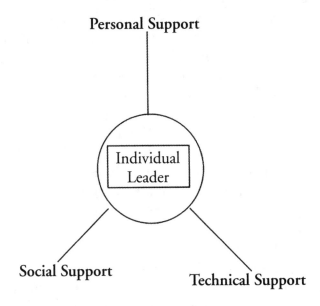

Social support comes from the relationships and contacts the leader develops with associates and colleagues within the organization. Social support can be experienced as one sits with committees, participates in activities of his or her profession, and generally gets acquainted with others in the process of carrying out the business of the church. As social beings, these informal networks satisfy a need for community and can provide information necessary to find further support. The social support Paul experienced was encouraging to him and brought great comfort (see Philippians 1:1-5).

Personal support comes from the more formal, yet focused relationships that the leader develops with other people in the organization. Personal support should be intentional and built into the organizational structure. It may be provided by assigned mentors, professional advisors, or others who take a personal interest in the leader and the work he or she is doing. Timothy, mentored by Paul, was guided in his development (see 1 Timothy 1:2-4). Personal support assists the leader in avoiding some of the pitfalls others have experienced. Personal support includes a listening ear and should include informal as well as formal counseling and advising. Personal support enhances performance within the organization. It may even be provided by individuals at a higher level within the church organization that have been assigned to "look out" for a new leader, to help him or her avoid some of the pitfalls others have experienced. Personal support provides the moral support, the listening ear, and the understanding that all individuals need in order to work well within organizations.

Technical, social, and personal support are especially meaningful to leaders when we consider that members of an organization are often shielded from the true weight of responsibility that a leader carries and often do not understand the tasks related to the position.

Let's consider a few facts about leadership before we attempt to suggest some practical ways to support leaders.

The leadership role

Context has much to do with a perception of what leadership approaches are deemed acceptable. Manfred Kets de Vries[3] in a book entitled *Leaders, Fools, and Impostors*, suggests that leadership is the exercise of power, and the quality of leadership—good, ineffective, or destructive—depends on an individual's ability to exercise power. When power is invested in leadership in the context of an authoritarian or dictatorial approach, leaders are seen as craving the opportunity to control people's actions, rather than as providing a valuable service. While the authoritarian approach may be appropriate in context of a crisis such as war or police or medical emergencies, leaders within the church who assume this perspective are misguided and likely to find a mismatch in the type of support they can expect.

Leaders must be aware of appropriate leadership style and context to be effective. According to Jay Conger[4], the leadership role can be conferred by followers, but they cannot be forced to grant it. This is especially true in voluntary associations such as churches, when members elect to join a congregation and often participate in the selection of those who serve in leadership positions. Think about how, in our own spiritual lives, God has given us the choice of electing to choose Him as our Sovereign Leader. If power in leadership within the church organization is patterned after that of Christ, we see servant leaders. Those who serve will attempt to mentor others to excellence rather than attempting to control or use others for personal gain.

General principles of leadership apply regardless of context, but they can be most effectively applied by taking context into account. For example, in health care, finance, and in business relations, persons in leadership positions are often advantaged by having a more complete knowledge of facts than those seeking their assistance. Even though an individual may have a general knowledge of health, when one visits a health care professional, one is usually seeking help, is willing to pay for it, and is thus more amenable to following professional, specialized advice. This is only partly the case in religious contexts. When church members serve in congregations or on church boards, they not only interact with leadership in a largely voluntary setting, but many who may be professionals themselves feel they have sufficient information to make their own decisions regardless of what a pastor proposes.

The culture of an organization may provide the impression that the sharing of information should flow only from leader to leader or from leader to subordinate, rather than the other way around. Individuals, and sometimes organizations, must overcome this misconception in order to develop a support network for leaders.

An organization would do well to develop creative ways to encourage leaders to take risks. As parents often do with young children, those new to leadership positions should to be given opportunities at an early point in their leadership life to make decisions in areas where the consequences of their decisions allow them to learn from the experience and yet not experience dire consequences should a poor decision be made. The framework for the new leader should be within a supportive environment designed to provide the opportunity for a positive experience. In this supportive environment leaders will be able to achieve positive growth when good decisions are made and to receive encouragement should poor decisions be made. Over time the number of good decisions should increase. It is primarily the encouragement a senior leader provides, both privately and publicly, that allows a new leader to develop.

Let us consider seven ways to support servant leaders.

Ways to support leaders

Persons in leadership positions are provided an opportunity to see things that others may not see. The opportunity to see the forest rather than the trees, so to speak, offers a different perspective on issues. Things often appear different from the top than from below. This explains why those in positions of leadership often act differently from the way they previously did or the way that they promised to act prior to assuming a leadership position. Their unanticipated actions as leader may not derive so much from a change of heart as from a change of perspective provided by information that is now available that was not available prior to their assuming the position of leadership.

Leaders must be able to view situations from a broad or holistic perspective, taking into account a range of possibilities available regarding decisions they must make. They must have enough information to take into account the consequences of their decisions to individuals and to the institution as a whole. Effective leaders seek information.

Thus, one practical way to provide support to a leader is to share information that will give perspective. Timely sharing of information is essential to be helpful, because it may provide additional options for consideration before decisions are made. Leaders can be spared many headaches through the sharing of information by others within the organization. Thus, support for leaders involves establishing processes for purposeful information sharing.

A second source of support relates to goal setting. Leaders are expected to develop and communicate clear and achievable goals. The development of clear and achievable goals helps a leader focus on priorities. In Christ's ministry on earth, He was purposeful and clear about His goals and the work He empowered His disciples to achieve (see Luke 5:1-11; Matthew 10:5-14). Assisting leaders with information and perspectives regarding the institution he or she is responsible to lead can make a difference in the ability to set goals and mentor others in achieving their potential. On a periodic basis leaders should be required to revisit previously established goals to determine whether priorities have changed.

Leaders are accountable for the tasks the role of leader requires. Thus, a third and essential support for leaders is feedback regarding the impact of institutional processes and decisions. Assisting leaders in establishing the information-decision-feedback loop provides a positive means for organizations to operate. This type of feedback may take various forms, including evaluations and surveys. Feedback provides another perspective that the leader would not otherwise have and can be of tremendous value.

Encouragement is a fourth source of support for those in leadership positions. Leaders are often in situations in which they must make difficult decisions based on information available to them that others may not have. Thus, they are frequently in a position to be misunderstood and/or criticized. Colin Munns[5] observes that one of the risks of leadership is isolation and the possibility of loneliness. A support structure is important in team functioning, according to James Whitehead and Evelyn Whitehead.[6] Organizations should purposefully seek opportunities to put these structures in place via professional or support networks, advisors, or other forms of support. Where support networks are lacking, a leader may feel uncomfortable sharing concerns with others. Offering a word of encouragement can ease the emotional and physical load leaders carry. Keep in mind that encouragement is what God provided to Christ in the Garden of Gethsemane and at other points in His ministry (see Luke 22:41-43; Matthew 3:16, 17). Discouragement is one of Satan's chief weapons. The importance of encouragement in a word or deed should not be overlooked.

Reserving judgment regarding leadership decisions until they have had sufficient time to take effect is a fifth form of support. Keep in mind that while leaders are involved in making decisions regarding current issues, much of their work is future oriented. Allow a leader sufficient time for decisions he or she has implemented to take place. The correctness of many of the decisions made by leaders cannot be adequately assessed until considerable time has elapsed since the original decision was made. It appears that Jesus' disciples were only able to truly assess the meaning of His ministry after He departed from them and went back to heaven.

Leaders need a time to renew their energies in order to avoid burnout. The constant challenge of being the point person and on stage can weigh heavily on the health and energies of leaders. A time away from the push and pull of organizational requirements can help to renew the energies that a leader needs in order to continue his or her productive work. Whether it is through planned retreats or through other means, organizations can assist a leader in the renewal process. Christ set the example by coming aside to rest from the crowds and the work He was doing. Thus, a sixth way to provide support for leaders is providing a time away from the normal work venue. A change of pace, an enrichment seminar, a brief trip away—all may provide an opportunity for relaxation and refreshment that provide a *time-out* period for leaders. This provides needed support for leaders.

Finally, rewards that reinforce and encourage can be a way of showing appreciation for the contribution that a person makes to an organization. Leaders should not be overlooked. Mary's expression of appreciation to Christ in anointing His feet was recognized by Christ as support and as an important affirmation of His leadership and care (see Luke 7:37, 38). Rewards are a seventh way to show support. They may be in a variety of forms, ranging from a note of encouragement, a small gift, a news note, or through a formal recognition process. The reason for the reward or recognition should not be obscure, and the intent should be genuine.

Not everyone is called upon to lead, nor will everyone who is called to lead accept such responsibility. Becoming a leader should not be a popularity contest; it should not be a game. Leaders are expected to provide *direction* for the group. Leadership requires charting a path for others to follow; it requires having a vision of what can be. Doing so requires a willingness to make tough decisions and even to lead in directions that may prove to be unpopular. Even though we do not always understand why a particular decision was made or agree with a decision that was made by a leader, those who accept the responsibility of leadership deserve our support.

The management of support is a vital process for the recruitment and retention of quality leaders. The advantages of providing support for leaders in church-affiliated institutions include personal and organizational benefits. We must keep in mind that leaders in our churches and institutions are human and subject to mistakes. They especially need support in the challenging times when decisions have not resulted in positive outcomes and mistakes are evident. Errors that some leaders make do not define their overall effectiveness in their service to the organization. To focus on errors alone is a disservice to the leader, his contribution, and the well-being of the organization. Response to the mistake should not destroy the opportunity for the person to provide meaningful service. The fact that leaders are subject to errors and mistakes is the very reason support processes are critical. Support may come from both formal and informal sources. Providing information, feedback, and encouragement to those in leadership positions are useful ways to nurture and retain effective leaders. In supporting our leaders using biblically based approaches, we provide opportunities for greater service to our church and community. Leadership within church organizations and their affiliated institutions is part of God's program of kingdom building.

C. Garland Dulan is director of the Education Department of the General Conference of Seventh-day Adventists in Silver Spring, Maryland.

[1] *Working Policy of the General Conference of Seventh-day Adventists*, 2002-2003 Edition (Hagerstown, Md.: Review and Herald Publishing Association), 29.

[2] Support for the Leaders, 2nd Forum on youth programme and adult resources, international team task, p. 4, found on <www.scout.org/europe/malaga2001/tt2.doc>.

[3] Manfred F. R. Kets de Vries, *Leaders, Fools, and Impostors* (San Francisco: Jossey-Bass, 1993), 22.

[4] Jay A. Conger, *Learning to Lead* (San Francisco: Jossey-Bass, 1992), 17.

[5] Colin Munns, "Developing a Strategy to Support Key Leaders," quoted in the Web site of the Leadership Learning Network, <http://www.leadership.ucaqld.com.au/cmunns.htm>.

[6] James Whitehead, Evelyn Whitehead, and John J. Egan, *The Promise of Partnership: A Model of Collaborative Ministry* (San Francisco: HarperSanFrancisco, 1993), 54, cited in Munns's article at <http://www.leadership.ucaqld.com.au/cmunns.htm>.

CHAPTER
13

Embracing
the World

Gary Krause

My wife and I weren't expecting to see such an unusual church parking lot in the middle of Pennsylvania's beautiful Amish farmlands. We were so surprised that we did a U-turn and drove back to take a closer look. Sure enough, on this Sunday morning, every one of the more than 200 vehicles parked in the lot—sedans, vans, trucks, pickups, and sports utility vehicles—was black.

There were no signs naming the church, but we guessed that it lay somewhere in the Amish or Mennonite tradition. Obviously the worshipers were more liberal than the traditional Amish (they worshiped in a church building and drove vehicles), but had strict rules about outward display (black vehicles only). We were amused to notice a few of the more sporty-looking cars had thin red stripes down the side. Perhaps some younger members of the congregation were trying to push the edge and their parents' patience.

The Christian church has always stood in tension with the world. We're not to love the world and its values (see 1 John 2:15), but Jesus died for the world because He loved it (see John 3:16). And His instruction is clear, that we should be in the world but "not of the world" (see John 17:15-17, NIV). Christians throughout history have struggled to find the correct balance. Some, such as the Amish, have played it safe by refusing to embrace the world for fear the world might embrace them. They live separate lives in separate communities. At the other extreme, some Christians have embraced so much of the world that their life, values, and priorities seem indistinguishable from those of anybody else.

How do we embrace the world with Christian love, showing the compassion of Jesus, without compromising? How do we share the good news with a world that so often doesn't want to listen? Not surprisingly, the key is found in the life and words of Jesus Himself.

The personal touch

Read the Gospels and you'll find Jesus telling practical, down-to-earth stories in the language of the people. He didn't remain aloof and distant. He was born in poverty, not in a palace. He mingled with the people rather than just sending instructions from heaven. His feet got covered in sand and His hands got dirty.

Jesus knew the value of the personal touch. "He went journeying from town to town and village to village, proclaiming the good news of the kingdom of God" (Luke 8:1, NEB). He did minister to large crowds. But just as often He was meeting a lone Nicodemus at night, talking with a woman in a Samaritan village, or touching a blind man's eyes.

Today we must use modern communication tools to spread the good news, and there's an important role for marketing and the media. But witness is not something that's done only by remote—by computers, machinery, satellites, or even professional public evangelists. It's something done by individual followers of Jesus as they try to walk in His path.

The foundation of Jesus' ministry was personal contact. Within decades after He went back to heaven, His message had spread throughout the then-known world. But it happened for one reason—the Master's hand had personally touched lives, and those lives personally touched others.

Today we can see the incarnational ministry of Jesus in the work of Global Mission pioneers. Since 1993, thousands of these lay Adventists, usually young people, have started most of the new Adventist congregations around the world. They've had amazing results in reaching out to people in parts of the world where the church previously had little or no success. In 1990 there were relatively few Adventists in the "10/40 window," for example.[1] Today church growth has exploded in that region.

Pioneers are indigenous people who live, eat, and work among their own culture. They understand the local language and ways of doing things, blend with the community, and communicate the love of Jesus through a holistic ministry. They've started hundreds of new churches in notoriously difficult areas such as northern India and West Africa.

Shaping our message to the world

On another Sunday morning, Bettina and I walked through the historic old town of Lewes, Delaware. All the restaurants and gift stores were closed—except a coffee shop doing a brisk trade.

Just a few yards farther down Second Street stood St. Peter's, a lovely Episcopal church consecrated in 1858. A small number of worshipers, bundled up against the cold, made their way through the church graveyard and into the sanctuary for the early service.

While worshipers at St. Peter's took Communion, patrons of the coffee shop drank coffee and ate sticky buns. While church attendees read from the Bible and the *Book of Common Prayer,* the coffee drinkers read the Sunday papers. The church echoed with hymns while in the coffee shop, classical music played quietly in the background.

It made me wonder. What are we doing as a church to embrace the people who are more comfortable sitting in a coffee shop than in a church? People who haven't opened a Bible in years, if at all?

A few years ago I visited Central Coast Community Church in New South Wales, Australia. It began as a church-planting project partly funded by Global Mission. I attended the children's Sabbath School— a loud, vibrant place with many children from non-Christian homes.

A little girl sitting beside me, who was restless and full of energy, suddenly raised her hand and called out, "How did Jesus die?"

"We'll talk about that later," replied the teacher.

With a big grin on her face the little girl said, "I hope he was shot."

In the busy noise of the room, the teacher missed the comment. But it hit me hard. I looked at the girl bouncing around in her chair. She had no idea about the life and death of Jesus. She'd probably only heard His name as an expletive. But now what she was learning in Sabbath School got all mixed up in her little head with the Hollywood action videos she no doubt watched at home.

We used to think of mission activities in terms of boys and girls in countries such as Burma, India, and China, who had never heard of Jesus. But now a whole generation of young Australians, New Zealanders, Americans, and Europeans has no knowledge of Jesus. Many have never heard of the Bible, let alone owned one.

The problem isn't so much that God is being attacked (which He is), but that He's being ignored. It's not so much a question of belief as it's a question of relevance. When you have clothes, food, a TV in the corner, and good times with your friends, the need for Jesus doesn't seem so urgent. In the West most of us are pretty happy "and have need of nothing" (see Revelation 3:17, KJV).

What are we doing to embrace this world? While the large cities have grown rapidly, the Adventist Church has remained largely rural. Reaching these urban people is one of the greatest challenges facing the church.

Perhaps now more than any other time in our church's history, we need to rediscover the incarnational ministry of Jesus. Now is the time for loving Adventists to mingle among the crowds and, like Jesus, have compassion on them. Now is the time for a holistic ministry, where we befriend those in our community and share the love of Jesus, not just through words but through actions.

Opening the doors

It's hard to imagine there was a time when Seventh-day Adventists in the United States (they existed nowhere else at first) believed that the gospel commission extended no farther than the Atlantic Ocean in the east, and the Pacific Ocean in the west.

Historian Richard Schwarz says that for the first quarter of a century after 1844, Adventists had "only a limited concept" of taking the good news to the entire world.[2] Migration made the United States an ethnic melting pot, and early Adventists thought they could go to every nation, kindred, tongue, and people without leaving the shores of the United States. It certainly seemed a more attainable goal for a small, young church facing a huge world. Arthur Spaulding says, "It was a comforting rationalization."[3]

But it wasn't long before the small group of believers crossed the Atlantic and Pacific oceans and began establishing the church in Asia, Africa, Europe, and the Pacific. An urgent belief that Jesus was coming soon fueled their mission fervor.

What about today? Do we still have a vision for embracing the entire world? If those early Adventists were resurrected today, they'd receive two major shocks. First, Jesus still hasn't come. Second, their "little flock" has become a worldwide denomination of nearly 14 million people, complete with the largest Protestant school system in the world, hospital networks, publishing houses and health food factories, media centers, and satellite television networks.

But would they find the same passion and vision for showing and sharing the love of Jesus with a world in need?

Sometimes we treat the church as an exclusive club in a gated housing community. We act like it's a place for members only, and those who don't conform to certain standards aren't welcome. It becomes a place where we look inward and focus on caring for our own wants, needs, and problems—and close the door on the world outside. How much time is spent on our church boards and in church business meetings focusing on our mission to the community? How much time do we spend praying and planning ways to embrace the world around us with God's love?

Søren Kierkegaard tells a story about a hospital where patients were dying like flies. Doctors panicked and scrambled for a cure, but nothing worked. The entire building was full of poison. Kierkegaard said this was like the state church in Denmark. Congregations were dying and everyone had a cure—a new hymn book, a different style of worship, a new altar book. But all was in vain. Spiritual poison was coming from the building itself and suffocating the whole organization. The church hadn't been ventilated, spiritually, for years.

How can we ventilate our church today? What's the antidote for spiritual poisoning? Perhaps we need to take hold of the church doors and windows and throw them open. Perhaps we need a fresh vision of our mission to reach our world with the love and compassion of Jesus.

Religious leaders attacked Jesus for breaking the rules of their club. They attacked Him for opening the doors and spending time with "publicans and sinners." They were right, of course. The Holy Son of God spent much of His time with bad people. What's even more amazing is that bad people wanted to spend time with Him. He was always at social gatherings. These people loved to be near Him. He never shut a door in their face.

You won't find any occasion where Jesus condemned a tax collector, a prostitute, or any other "sinner," but you will find occasions where He condemned the religious leaders. He said, "They tie up heavy loads and put them on men's shoulders" (Matthew 23:4). He said, "Woe to you, teachers of the law and Pharisees, you hypocrites! You shut the kingdom of heaven in men's faces" (Matthew 23:13).

Acceptance doesn't mean going easy on sin. It simply means we don't throw the first stone. Even though Jesus knew the power of sin intimately, He was a friend to sinners. He opened doors to them. As a church we can't afford to shut our doors and form a club of people who just sing nice songs, listen to wonderful sermons, have sweet fellowship—and just wait for Jesus to come. What about our world? What about being salt? What about being light?

We can't see through shut doors. We can't see the millions of people who don't know Jesus. We can't see people in our community who are suffering. We can't see injustice and cruelty. We lose any vision of going *into* the entire world.

Translating the message

How do we go into the entire world? Are we like messengers leaving the church fortress in the morning and then scurrying back to its safety at night? Jesus used quite different descriptions of His followers. We are to be like "light," "salt," and "yeast"—mingling, permeating, influencing. But how can we even begin to share with people who have such radically different backgrounds, worldviews, beliefs, and values?

In some ways our witness can be likened to Digital Video Disks (DVDs), which are coded according to world region. DVDs manufactured in the United States and Canada are coded Region 1, while the code for China is Region 6, and the code for Europe is Region 4. Hold a Region 6 code DVD in one hand and a Region 1 code DVD in the other and you can't tell the difference. But if you try to play a Region 1 code DVD in a Region 6 code DVD player, the images will be distorted, and you won't hear the audio properly.

Homeland translation

On Second Street in Lewes, Delaware, we saw two radically different cultures operating—one represented by the café, and one represented by the church. As Adventists, we've done reasonably well in sharing our faith with people from the church culture. But we've done poorly in embracing those represented by the café culture.

How do we move outside our church boundaries to embrace this world? Perhaps, like DVDs, our message needs to be translated into terms the people we're trying to reach can understand. Perhaps we need to learn the languages and cultures of people in our own society, before we can share the good news effectively.

We can speak as we have always spoken, but people may not listen. We can share books we've always shared, but they may not be the sort of books these people will read or understand. We can preach as we've always preached, but these people may not stay around to listen.

We can give the trumpet a certain sound and speak the truth with conviction. We can confidently proclaim the complete 27 Fundamental Beliefs. But like a Region 1 code DVD in a Region 6 code DVD player or an English-speaking pastor in the jungles of Africa—if the people don't listen or understand, we haven't communicated.

Our task as Adventists is to translate—to convert eternal principles in the Adventist message into people's immediate context. It means leading into our message through *their* mind-set and circumstances, not *our* mind-set and circumstances. It means exploring *their* culture, not placing *our* culture on them. It means discovering *their* interests, which may not always be *our* interests.

Of course, over the years Christian missionaries have consistently looked for aspects of local culture that they can use to direct people to Jesus. Paul and Caroline Richardson worked among the Sawi people of Papua New Guinea and found it hard to tell the gospel story because the Sawi saw treachery as a virtue. They saw Judas, not Jesus, as the hero.

Seemingly thwarted, the Richardsons then discovered that the Sawi made peace by having a father in each of the warring villages give one of their children as a peace child to their enemies. Immediately they saw the opportunity to tell the gospel story in terms the people could understand—Jesus the Peace Child given by the loving Father.

Pastor Frank Maberly, Adventist missionary to Papua New Guinea, tells of meeting with a tribe that revered ten sacred stones. He used these stones as a vehicle to tell them about the Ten Commandments.

We can easily appreciate why missionaries have needed to take these approaches overseas, but for many of us it's a novel concept that we might need to do exactly the same thing for the neighbor next door.

Of course, as soon as we start trying to reach our world through their interests, and share our message in different ways, and in terms that we don't normally use, we should be ready for criticism. We will be accused of "diluting the truth." We'll be accused of eroding our fundamental beliefs.

On one occasion I was sitting in church listening to the sermon when a woman immediately behind me started whispering loudly to the person next to her. I found it distracting as I was trying to listen to the preacher. I resisted the temptation of looking around.

Then I noticed she wasn't speaking in English. *That would be right*, I thought. *Thinks she can get away with it because nobody can understand what she's saying.* The space in the pew directly in front of me was vacant, and I considered quietly slipping into it. *But she might know it's because of her, and I don't want to give offense.*

I was feeling quite self-righteous, of course. My motivation was purely spiritual—I wanted to concentrate on what the pastor was saying. And then it suddenly hit me. This woman was whispering because she was translating the sermon for the person next to her.

Naturally I felt about two inches high.

When we start the task of embracing the world and building bridges to people outside our walls, there will be times that we see and hear things that we might think are out of place, annoying, or different from the way we normally do things. Some of us would be shocked to see Adventists in Burma chanting their way through Sabbath School—until they realize they're reciting lengthy sections of Scripture about the Second Coming. The message hasn't been changed, it's just been translated into terms that people understand and appreciate.

Of course this is not new or radical or untried. It's exactly the method used by Jesus. He shaped the good news into words and actions that people would understand. When visiting a farming community, He told stories about wheat, about animals, about sowing seed. It's also the method used by the apostle Paul, who determined to "become all things to all men so that by all possible means I might save some" (1 Corinthians 9:22). Thus, the way he spoke to Jewish people (see, for example, Acts 9:19-22) was very different from the way he approached pagans (see, for example, Acts 14:15-17 and Acts 15).

And notice the various word pictures the New Testament uses to describe salvation. They include adoption (Romans 8:15); redemption (1 Peter 1:18, 19); reconciliation (Romans 5:10); justification (Galatians 2:16); liberation (Romans 6:18); marriage (Romans 7:2-4); inheritance (Romans 8:17); forgiveness (Luke 1:76, 77); and being found (Luke 15). The Bible writers obviously had no problem with expressing the truth (which doesn't change) in different ways to be meaningful to different audiences.

Each word picture is referring to the same truth of Jesus' death on the cross, but each is expressed in different terms and might be more meaningful to certain people, at certain times in certain places. Paul's metaphors of redemption and justification had a particular resonance for people steeped in the Roman system of law. Perhaps Jesus' story of the prodigal son may have resonance for a postmodern society, in which people know what it's like to feel lost.

Matching the method to the need

The most impressive witness is often given without words—the eloquent testimony of, in Ellen White's words, a "loving and lovable Christian" (*The Ministry of Healing*, 470). Sometimes, people's "hearts may be as hard as the beaten highway, and apparently it may be a useless effort to present the Saviour to them." But, she adds, "while logic may fail to move, and argument be powerless to convince, the love of Christ, revealed in personal ministry, may soften the stony heart, so that the seed of truth can take root" (*Gospel Workers*, 185). A church's inner-city soup kitchen for the homeless can be a more powerful testimony than an evangelistic seminar in the church sanctuary. When Jesus embraced the world He cared for people's physical as well as their spiritual needs.

Effective outreach always matches the medicine to the wounds. A missionary in Africa does not begin his or her ministry with a lecture on Daniel's prophecies. A worshiping-on-Friday Muslim may not be much interested in a lecture on why Saturday rather than Sunday is the Sabbath. An atheistic investment banker in New York City who doesn't believe the Bible will not be convinced of truth by an in-depth Bible study with 500 convincing texts.

I can put together a witnessing package—put in a few doctrines, a few Bible verses—and then pass it on to a secular person. There's nothing wrong with the message. It's truth. It's all perfectly correct. But there's a major problem. Like a Regional Code 1 DVD in a Regional Code 6 DVD player, communication is not effective if the recipients don't understand what they've been given.

Ellen White puts it this way: "The apostle [Paul] varied his manner of labor, shaping his message to the circumstances under which he was placed." She adds, "The laborer for God is to study carefully the best methods," and workers are "not to be one-idea men, stereotyped in their manner of working, unable to see that their advocacy of truth must vary with the class of people among whom they work and the circumstances they have to meet" (*Gospel Workers*, 118, 119).

In other words, let's put Code 1 DVDs in Code 1 DVD players.

We should not make it difficult

In the Book of Acts, Luke reports on a big conference of church leaders who gathered to discuss a major challenge they were facing. The early Christians, of course, were basically Jews who had discovered that Jesus was the Messiah. But soon a growing number of people from outside the Jewish faith were starting to take an interest in Christianity.

So the leaders faced the challenge of how best to incorporate people from a totally different background into the new Christian church. The discussion at the conference is fascinating, but perhaps the most important speech was given by James—probably Jesus' brother. He concluded: "It is my judgment, therefore, that we should not make it difficult for the Gentiles who are turning to God" (Acts 15:19).

James wasn't suggesting that the leaders "water down" the message. He wasn't suggesting they compromise truth. He was suggesting—actually, he was downright pleading—that the church open up its doors, make the message relevant, and do everything it could to make it easy for people to become Christians.

When Jesus came to this world, He gave the ultimate demonstration of embracing the world. He left His own context and merged Himself fully with humanity—in human skin, in a human family. He never compromised His Divinity, but became one with us.

Are we prepared to open the doors and move outside our cultural comfort zones for the sake of others? It's our mission, should we choose to accept it.

Gary Krause is the husband of Bettina, his greatly loved best friend, and is communication director for the office of Global Mission at the General Conference of Seventh-day Adventists.

---

[1] The 10/40 window is an area stretching from West Africa through the Middle East and into Asia. Here live the majority of the world's population, the world's poorest people, and the fewest Christians.

[2] Richard W. Schwarz, *Light Bearers to the Remnant* (Nampa, Idaho: Pacific Press, 1979), 141.

[3] Arthur W. Spaulding, *Origin and History of Seventh-day Adventists* (Hagerstown, Md.: Review and Herald, 1962), 2:193.